1/2    # 8⁵⁰

Michael Boyny

# FROM ALASKA
# TO TIERRA DEL FUEGO

With love to Sabine

Michael Boyny

# FROM ALASKA TO TIERRA DEL FUEGO

## Across the Americas in Two Years

B BUCHER

# Contents

# This much is certain: travel is always a good thing.

So said Voltaire, and we agree with him. However, it can't be denied that travel is a dangerously addictive drug. This view will instantly be understood by anyone who has a passion for hanging out at railway stations, airports or highway rest stops, not because they're actually traveling, but simply because those places are redolent of far-flung places and being on the road. Or is traveling an instinct, perhaps? Because after all, aren't we all nomadic by nature? Are we really wanderers, not designed for settling down to a sedentary life? Personally, I sympathize with this theory, which would give our obsession a veneer of genetic legitimacy...! It was in 1992 that my wife Sabine and I undertook our first journey together which went beyond the confines of a summer vacation. We toured the remote outback of Australia in an all-terrain vehicle, and there, in the clear starry nights somewhere between the Simpson and Tanami deserts, we divined that this experience would prove to be the opening page to a new chapter of our lives. We began planning our next large-scale tour straight away in the airplane back to gray old Germany. And this continued for the next eight years: the intervals between our extended travels primarily served the purpose of collecting enough money and enough reasons to set off again. I became a photographer, choos-

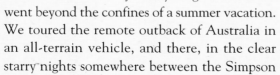

... don't want to grow up ...!

A compact collection: Lucy's parlor, decorated with souvenirs from four continents

ing a profession which dramatically simplified the reasons issue at least. We produced slide shows and toured them through Germany (more traveling, in other words), recounting our experiences in venues from Hamburg in the north to Lake Constance in the south.

At some stage we decided it was time to grow up, and cut back our travel to more conventional levels. Sabine opened a pottery workshop and I set up a photography studio; we moved into an apartment in the center of Munich, decorated it with our souvenirs from foreign countries and thought we'd settled down. But … it didn't work. One gray winter evening in January 2003 I was surfing listlessly on the Internet and came across a website showing a young couple driving down the Panamericana in an old mail bus. And there it was again, the old familiar itch. I felt like a recovered alcoholic who'd bitten into a liqueur chocolate by mistake (which would confirm the addiction theory). I hauled my old world atlas down from the bookshelf and traced the couple's route with my finger, already imagining myself on deserted muddy

tracks in the mountain cloud forest of Costa Rica ... and it took little effort to draw Sabine into my fantasies.

We'd soon devised a detailed plan. We would drive from Alaska to Tierra del Fuego in our own truck, an adventure taking us through fifteen countries; we would complete the journey in two years and reckon with a further two for advance preparations. It was the start of exciting weeks and months in which we spent the majority of our free time at the computer or in travel bookstores. And above all, we needed a third member for our team, a suitable vehicle: with four-wheel drive, rugged diesel engine and comfortable living quarters; a vehicle of a make that was common in as many countries as possible along our route to simplify the search for spare parts, and one which would not overtax our budget ... an extensive list of requirements which considerably limited our choices on the market. But we found just what we were looking for. On the Internet, on mobile.de: Lucy! An indefatigable old 1985 US Ford F250 pick-up mounted with a brand-new motorhome cab, 6.9 liter V8 direct injection engine and no elec-

tronic bells and whistles – just honest, resilient rough-and-ready action, rugged chassis, comfortable superstructure, affordable and ... gorgeous! It was a little like responding to a lonely hearts ad. Following a hunch, we bought the old lady on the spot, dizzy with happiness; we souped her up and devotedly redecorated her living quarters.

The "dress rehearsal" for our journey took place in the summer of 2004. We planned a six-week tour heading for the North Cape through Norway and returning through Finland. But our test drive ended around 200 kilometers (120 miles) north of the Arctic Circle near the little backwater of Fauske, with major transmission damage....! The show can only be a success if the dress rehearsal is a disaster, said my drama teacher at school. And she was always right.

We were on the right track ...

*Left: A bungalow with veranda: parking site at a "palapa" in Baja California, Mexico*
*Bottom: A great team at Salar de Uyuni, Bolivia.*

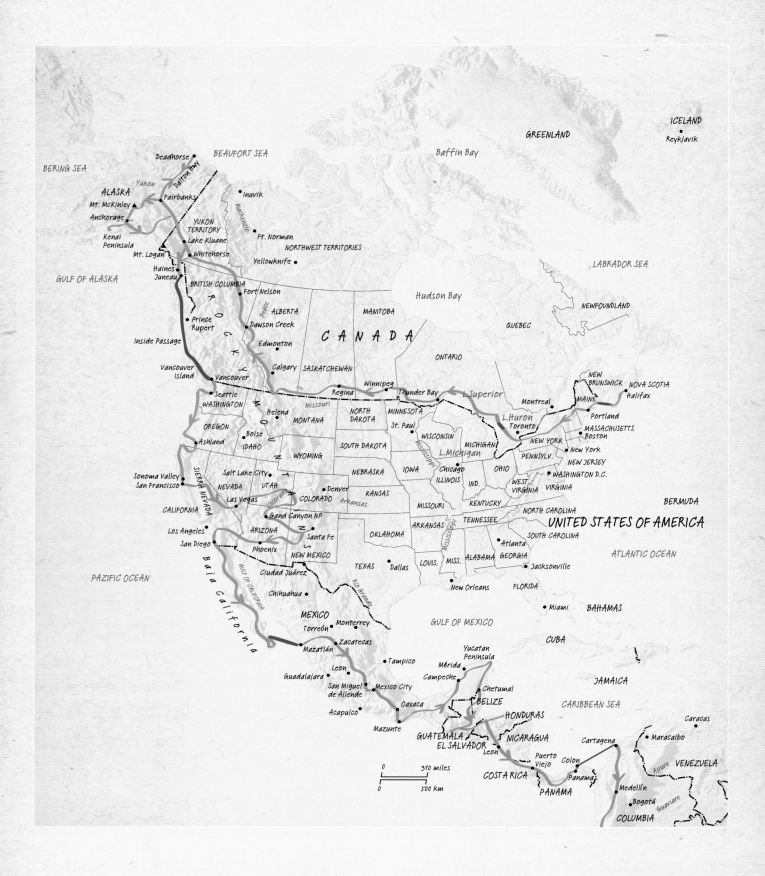

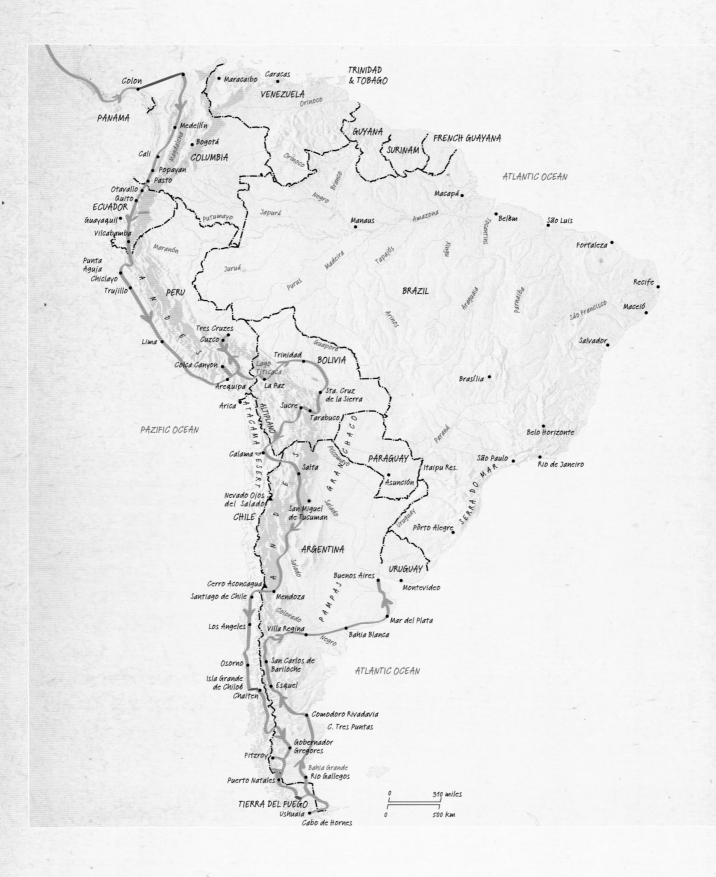

The king of canyons – the Grand Canyon

# Departure: On the road!

*"Even the longest journey begins with the first step. Take pleasure in it – you will stumble on the second."*
*Chinese proverb*

[km 0/mile 0 | Munich – Boston]

*Do they have this in Bolivia ...?*

We have spent two years preparing for this journey, making plans, drawing up routes, buying a suitable vehicle and the equipment we will need. We pored over the computer for nights on end, combing the furthest-flung corners of the Web for useful information, building castles in the air and pondering over probably marginal issues such as whether it's possible to find a good espresso in Bolivia (and I bet there's an Internet forum somewhere with the answer). We visited countless official departments and doctors' practices, and amassed a mountain of travel literature of positively Alpine proportions as the months went by. Now, on this sunny Sunday in May, we are finally about to depart. The imminent departure causes butterflies in our stomachs. We sit with friends on the terrace of our corner tavern and drink a final Munich wheat beer accompanied by an order of the local veal sausage specialty, secretly wondering whether we'll be able to find it in Bolivia too. Later we all embrace and agree, while saying our farewells, to meet up in the beer garden in two years' time. We rev up Lucy's eight cylinders, honk the district out of its midday snooze, wave until our arms ache and drive off. Turn into Ehrengutstrasse, along the River Isar to the ring road and from there onto the north-bound highway. We're on the road! From now on, we'll be traveling for two years from Alaska to Tierra del Fuego, roaming through foreign lands like nomads, exploring primeval country far off the beaten track and discovering unknown cultures, leaving a comfortable, secure life behind us to seek adventure. No telephone, no appointments, no traffic jams, no haste, no stress, no compromises – but lots of different kinds of beer. In drizzly Bremerhaven we hand Lucy over to the shipping company. She disappears for three weeks into the dark belly of the "Atlantic Conveyor", which will take her across the Atlantic to Halifax in Canada. Three weeks in which we plan to take the time to explore America's east coast. We take the train to Hamburg, spend our last night in Europe in a sterile room in the airport hotel, sleeping little, and board a flight for New York the next day. America, here we come!

Around 5 pm, our plane lands at Newark Airport, New Jersey, 26 kilometers (15.5 miles) from Manhattan. After the arduous immigration process, we treat ourselves to a quick espresso at Starbucks. The coffee-colored beauty behind the counter starts to apply a lid to the coffee cup. "It's okay," I assure her, "I'm drinking it here." Her expression freezes and she informs me in severe tones that she has to put the lid on because the coffee is hot and I might spill it, scald myself and sue Starbucks. Welcome to the United States of America! Our filthy Chevy taxi edges across twelve-lane highways in the

Top and left:
We'll miss each other:
saying goodbye to our
neighbors.

"America, here we come!"

evening rush-hour of the eight-million-inhabitant metropolis. Although the dreadlocked African-American driver tries to act cool, he appears on the verge of a nervous breakdown at every new traffic jam. We progress at a snail's pace, and soon grow concerned about our driver's wellbeing. Lincoln Tunnel swallows us on the New Jersey side and spits us out into the gorges of Manhattan. Here the traffic is at a complete standstill; our driver is on the point of collapse. He's definitely in the wrong job.

Our journey ends on 34th and Broadway, where we move into a gloomy apartment on the third floor of Harold Building, overlooking to the yard to the rear – which is only a little larger than a bath towel and hemmed in by twenty-eight floors. Only a trickle of daylight reaches our plain room.

The next seven days are spent roaming tirelessly through Manhattan. We visit the Statue of Liberty, Ellis Island, the Museum of Modern Art, a Broadway musical and the Empire State Building. We drift through trendy Greenwich Village, bustling Times Square and lively Chinatown before sinking exhausted onto a bench in tranquil Central Park. On Broadway, we walk our feet off and then recover in gorgeous gourmet temples in SoHo. We are seduced and occasionally confused by this mega-city that makes a virtue out of immoderation and whose inhabitants elevate self-promotion to an art form of the highest order. Perhaps the lonely gas station attendant, whom we encounter some weeks later in Vermont, is right when he says that you either love New York or hate it. We have no doubt that we belong to the first category, but take care to move on after a week. Too much New York is like too much Starbucks coffee!

In the suburb of Tappan on the other side of the Hudson, at a Swiss car rental company, we take possession of a brand-new camper van with all the conveniences Americans expect from an

RV: over 7 meters (23 feet) long, generous double bed, fully equipped kitchen with four-burner stove, oven and microwave, optional sound/TV system and of course shower, toilet and bowling alley in the rear. We will be touring New England for a week in this fortress, bowling along deserted highways from New Jersey and New York to Connecticut, through rolling hills and deep forests, past pretty towns with names like Poughkeepsie, Canaan and Mystic. Spacious houses with impressive verandas indicate considerable prosperity, and stand in neatly tended gardens in which friendly people wave to each other. At least three cars stand in front of each double garage, all brand-new and sparkling clean. The town centers are dominated by whitewashed wooden churches with pointed spires that are characteristic of New England, and are otherwise crammed with art galleries next to antique stores rubbing shoulders with cafés next to more art galleries... We drive through a smart, scrubbed world, pretty

*Left page, top:*
*Blue hour over*
*Manhattan.*
*top left and bottom*
*right: All the city's a*
*stage: New York.*

Strolling on Cape Cod beach

and morally irreproachable. In Massachusetts we head for Cape Cod, a peninsula extending into the Atlantic like a slim bent arm. At its furthermost tip, the little town of Provincetown clings to the isthmus. We stay there for a few days, immersing ourselves in an America that's refreshingly different. The town is beautifully situated between the stretches of ocean, its houses painted in shades of bright pink, blue and turquoise and festooned not only with the obligatory Stars and Stripes, but also with flags in rainbow shades: Provincetown is a bastion of gay culture. Male couples walk hand in hand down Commercial Street, casting suggestive glances in my direction. The galleries exhibit wood carvings of athletic bodies with enormous erect penises –

Sabine sketches them busily …as inspiration for her pottery, she claims just a touch too casually. What a wonderfully subversive contrast to the often sterile moral climate outside the town's boundary. We browse through salacious bookstores and boutiques where the air is dense with incense, "inspiring" galleries and a scrumptious culinary scene; we hire bicycles and explore the surrounding dunes, sitting on the beach for hours and gazing at the expanse of deep blue sea. We spend carefree days in Provincetown and place the town high up on our "I could live here" list. Finally we set off for Boston, where we return the RV. We're eager to be rid of it. Not that we're complaining; New York was fascinating, our trip through New England was beautiful and traveling in this comfortable American "condo on wheels" was downright luxurious, but we've had enough. It's time for us to return to our shelter, to feel Lucy's rough diesel jouncing us along, and to embark on our journey to the destination that our girl on wheels was designed for – the wilderness!

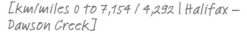

# Canada: The Long Road West

"Two roads diverged in a wood, and I – I took the one less traveled by, and that has made all the difference."

*Robert Frost, American poet*

[km/miles 0 to 7,154 / 4,292 | Halifax – Dawson Creek]

*Full of pride: Canadian scout in Fort McCleod, Alberta.*

There's no doubt that Canada is an absolutely gigantic country. When I unfold the map of the world in my address book and place a ruler between Halifax, on Canada's east coast, and Anchorage, the capital of Alaska, the distance between them is 5.8 centimeters (2.3 inches). When I measure 5.8 centimeters (2.3 inches) from the south of Munich using the same map, I end up somewhere on the borders of Botswana and South Africa. It's mid-June, we're on the east coast and the Alaskan summer is brief, so we don't plan to waste any time.

In Boston we board a small aircraft to Halifax in the province of Nova Scotia, where we take a plain but cheap room in the Bayview Motor Inn not far from the harbor. The "Atlantic Conveyor", in the hold of which Lucy has been traveling for the past twenty days, docked this evening – we can actually see it from our motel room. The next two days are taken up by the formalities necessary before we can reclaim our vehicle. We shuttle back and forth, arms filled with customs and freight documents, between the shipping office, the harbor and the customs office. Although occasionally confusing, the whole business is far smoother than we had feared. The handover takes place on a cloudy Wednesday evening. Lucy stands in the wan light of the docks, and I'd swear she's smiling as

we come closer. The rear lock box has been broken into and our tools, a waterproof tarpaulin and my beloved battery screwdriver have been stolen. May the thief mash his fingers with the hammer – which he also stole!

We take one more day to prepare thoroughly for the start of our journey, buying new tools, filling the gas bottles and packing provisions into the spare crate before we finally set off on this 5.8-cm-long road to Alaska. We follow the Lighthouse Route toward Yarmouth along bumpy coastal roads, past deeply cleft, craggy bays, some with white sand, passing sleepy villages that speak of old stories about smugglers, sunken ships and treasure, and encountering relaxed people with refreshingly dry, friendly ways. At the south-western tip of Nova Scotia we board the ferry for Bar Harbour, Maine, USA. We're facing our first border crossing into the United States with Lucy. What horror stories we've read in the past few months, about harmless tourists who wanted to travel to the USA in their own vehicles and were turned back at the border for outlandish reasons: the vehicle looks too military, the driver's name appears on some dubious list of "undesirables" or the passenger's haircut doesn't conform to the standards! But nothing of the kind happens this time; our crossing into Maine is swift and friendly. No un-

necessary questions, no demand for an inventory of the vehicle contents, no search of the living quarters; in fact, I'm not even asked to remove my hat for an inspection of my haircut (which would have been our shakiest point). It rains plenty in Maine, New Hampshire and Ver-

mont. Because of this we take only short breaks, so that after only a few days we're back at the Canadian border – this time at its most spectacular point: Niagara Falls.

As quoted in our guidebook, Oscar Wilde once remarked acrimoniously that "Niagara Falls is simply a vast amount of water going the wrong way over some unnecessary rocks; the sight of that waterfall must be one of the earliest and keenest disappointments in American married life." Isn't that a little unfair? After all, around 250,000 cubic meters of water per second roar over the 675-meter-wide (2214 feet) cliffs at Horseshoe Falls, tumbling 54 meters (177 feet) to stillness below. The statistics are impressive – and we're certainly stunned as we stand at the rail and gaze at the thundering wall of water. But it's also true that every drop of that

*Top: Early summer on Lake Louise in Jasper National Park, Alberta.*
*Left: Construction on the Trans Canada Highway.*

19

water, right down to the last molecule, seems to have been appropriated for an abysmal marketing campaign. Commercialism has adopted particularly abstruse forms on the Canadian side, where the casino, waxworks, Honeymoon City Motel, Ripley's "Believe It Or Not" museum, several "houses of horror" and countless stores, fast-food restaurants, discos and so on cluster near the Falls.

We are sobered, almost repulsed by the slick manner in which the throngs of visitors around the natural spectacle itself are processed. Was Mr. Wilde right after all? Not quite: our trip in the "Maid of the Mist", a solid diesel launch that takes us close to the falls amid the spray, is literally oceans of fun. Everyone on the trip is handed a blue raincoat – thank heavens; not because they're so stylish, but because otherwise the mighty Falls soak you to the skin. We spend the whole sunny day at this place, once a secret

site for First Nations people. And although we don't fall to our knees in awe like Father Louis Hennepin, the first white man to set eyes on the cliffs in 1678 (albeit still in their unspoilt natural state), we do agree that the Niagara Falls are well worth a visit.

We traverse the elongated Bruce Peninsula which extends into mighty Lake Huron and soon reach the Trans Canada Highway, or – as the people here respectfully call it – the TCH. It crosses Canada from St. John's in far eastern Newfoundland to Victoria on Vancouver Island, the westernmost tip of the country.

The TCH is said to be 7,500 to 8,000 kilometers (4,500 to 4,800 miles) long, although nobody around here knows its exact length. All along its middle stretch – for example, the section of the highway in western Ontario north of Lake Superior, that is, precisely at the point where we join the route – the TCH still cuts

through virtually uninhabited wilderness. In fact it's the only road to connect the east of Canada with the west, and wasn't built until the early 1960s. Before this time, driving from Halifax to Vancouver on Canadian roads had been impossible, and the journey had involved a detour via the United States. Our plan to more or less keep to this highway until we reach the Canadian Rockies is not too successful, the problem being the spectacular scenery at the early stages of our route.

... Yellow – the fashion hit

The isolated road continually encounters steep, rocky cliffs or the deserted sandy banks of Lake Superior, a lake which is so enormous that we have the feeling we are driving along beside the ocean itself instead of inland waters. For long stretches no land is in sight on the other side, and the lake actually has tides, albeit modest ones. At Lake of the Woods in the far west of Province of Ontario, we make an unplanned stop, set up camp directly on the shore, unpack our canoe from the roof of the van and paddle through the cool waters.

We discover deserted wooded banks and little uninhabited islands in the lake. And when our provisions are low, we steer for the next general store in Sioux Narrows – a two-hour paddle away – feeling just like old trappers out of a

*Above: Too cold to swim – a secluded lake in Waterton National Park, Alberta.*
*Right: Destination wilderness – overnight camp in the Canadian Rockies.*

James Fennimore Cooper novel. We've arrived in the wilderness!

We gradually leave the rolling hills of the lake country behind and plunge into the endless prairies of Manitoba, Saskatchewan and Alberta. Straight as a die, the TCH leads west through never-ending ochre-hued fields of grain.

The road carries us along, and we make up the time we have lost. In Regina, the spry capital of Saskatchewan province, we stop for two days while Lucy receives her first service and we take the opportunity to have a new brake servo unit fitted. Our old lady purrs reliably along, sailing easily through the vastness of the country. She's slow to start on chilly mornings – but goodness, so are we!

Finally we see the Canadian Rockies rising to the west. In Waterton National Park, near the US border, we reach their foothills and now head north, switching to the rough, dusty track of the Forestry Trunk Road, twisting and turn-

ly praised as Canada's most beautiful mountain route, and certainly much of the scenery is absolutely breathtaking. But our seclusion is at an end. We tag onto an endless convoy of RVs and wonder just how much tourism a wilderness can take. 500 meters (1,640 feet) from the parking lot down a hiking trail, however, the situation looks better, things are quieter. Walking is not a popular American pastime (we've seen campers who drive the 150 meters (492 feet) to the shower block), so avoiding the crowds is rather easy for us.

We ramble through deep forests alongside rushing streams and toil up stony paths to craggy heights, where we are rewarded with spectacular views. The dramatic beauty of this mountain world stirs us profoundly.

One peak bears a sign which commands us, "You are just a few steps from the summit. Enjoy the view, but also enjoy the personal feeling of knowing that you are a part of this landscape." We understand.

*Above: Stormy clouds pursue us in Waterton National Park.*
*Left: An idyllic place for a break.*

ing up to heights over 2,000 meters (6,560 feet). A dramatic panorama unfurls before us, with snow-capped peaks, boundless forests, crystalline rivers and milky turquoise mountain lakes – a jewel of creation.

However, the numbers of tourists we encounter are growing. At the little town of Banff we join the Icefields Parkway which spans the entire length of Banff and Jasper National Parks. These 230 kilometers (138 miles) are frequent-

Solitary angler on Lake Kluanc, Yukon

# Alaska – into the Wild

"The Promised Land always lies on the other side of a Wilderness."
*Havelock Ellis, British sexual psychologist and social reformer*

[km/miles 7,154/4,292 to 14,534/8,720|
Dawson Creek – Haines]

*Above: Can't miss it – the starting point of the Alaska Highway in Dawson Creek. Bottom right: Pink Mountain Roadhouse, providing travelers with longed – for hot showers.*

When the Japanese attacked Pearl Harbor on December 7, 1941, the Americans, fearing an invasion of the far north, planned a supply road to help in defending Alaska. On February 11, 1942, President Roosevelt issued the command to build a highway through impassable wilderness, endless forest, mosquito-infested swamps and steep, craggy mountains – the birth of the Alaska Highway. The task was taken up by almost 11,000 men, toiling through the inhospitable north with all the tools and manpower they could muster, and was completed by November 20, 1942. An incredible feat! A little over six months to complete the main work required for 2,230 kilometers (1,338 miles) of highway! The starting-point of the Alaska Highway is Dawson Creek, clearly marked by a monstrous gateway at the visitor center parking lot. It is surrounded by the usual conglomeration of functional single-storey buildings housing fast-food restaurants, car dealerships and supermarkets. Not an agreeable place, so that we curtail our stopover to the minimum, driving through the gateway, taking the obligatory souvenir photo and setting out on our long route north.

Just after Dawson Creek the weather takes a turn for the worse. It starts to rain – in fact, it pours. After around 100 kilometers (60 miles) on a well-kept but deserted road through woods and farmland, the windshield wiper begins to make a strange squeaking noise. After a further hundred kilometers (60 miles) it stops working intermittently, and shortly before we reach the hamlet of Fort Nelson 150 kilometers (90 miles) later, it finally gives up for good. I dismantle the windshield wiper motor (in the pouring rain, of course), cross the road to a little spare parts store and ask for a wiper motor for a 1985 F250. The eccentric salesman disappears behind a curtain and seconds later pushes exactly the same model across the counter towards me. We're definitely driving the right kind of vehicle. A sign at the entrance to the hamlet seems to confirm our view. "This is Ford Country – what are you driving?" The most spectacular scenery along the Alaska Highway can be found just north of Fort Nelson, where the northern foothills of the Rockies encircle a narrow valley, towering over Stone Mountain Provincial Park. The road

snakes through a limestone gorge where mountain goats block the narrow serpentine curves; further north, we spot bison at the roadside. A black bear ambles over the gray asphalt before our eyes and vanishes into the dense gloom of the forest before I can lift the camera to my eye. Wild, rugged country – beautiful, yet only a foretaste of what awaits us far to the north. Our next stop is Watson Lake in Yukon Province, aside from Whitehorse, the only town in this 1,000 kilometer (600 miles) stretch that boasts what one might almost describe as complete infrastructure. (Aren't these glorious names, invoking tales of adventure and life in the wilderness in the far north? Here are some others in the same vein: Sixtymile, Klondike River, Coldfoot, Livengood, and my absolute favorite: Deadhorse!). Watson Lake is a backwater with little charm, and would hardly be worth stopping for except to buy gas if it weren't for the signposts. "Sign Post Forest" is an extensive, conspicuous collection of wooden posts along the highway to

which visitors from all over the world have nailed fingerposts, car license plates, signposts and a whole host of other kinds of sign. The collection was started in 1942 by Carl K. Lindley, a homesick soldier from Danville, Illinois, who erected a signpost pointing the way to his hometown. His example was followed by other laborers and truck drivers, and later by hosts of tourists. The colorful collection of curiosities currently numbers over 50,000.

In Whitehorse we have our first encounter with the Yukon River. In the late 19th century, the town became an important stopping point for prospectors on their way to Dawson City; from here, the river is navigable up to its estuary at the Bering Sea. Today, around 24,000 people live here – representing two-thirds of the entire population of Yukon. We stroll through the pretty town, find a cozy café where we are served an unexpectedly delicious lunch, and stock up on provisions in the gigantic supermarket. The range of produce here in the far north

*The most spectacular landscapes on the Alaska Highway are found outside Fort Nelson.*

27

*Breathtaking solitude along the last few kilometers on Canadian soil.*

is astonishing – fresh giant prawns and Australian Rosemount Estate Chardonnay for 12.99 Canadian dollars instead of 15.99. In the evening, we stand on the banks of crystalline Lake Kluane, delighting in the view across the mirror-smooth waters to the mountains and feasting like (Canadian) kings.

The final section of the Alaska Highway on the Canadian side is in terrible shape. It runs through mountainous country and dense coniferous forests scarred by river courses with narrow rivulets flowing through their wide beds and named Domjek River, Kluane River or White River. Now, in early August, the rivers are almost dry, but in the brief fall season the rains increase. In winter the rivers freeze and expand, only to thaw in spring and carve these huge gashes through the landscape.

In Beaver Creek we refill all our tanks before finally crossing the border to Alaska on the sixth of August. The first part of our journey is behind us; since leaving Halifax, we've traveled almost 10,000 kilometers (6,000 miles) in forty-three days, negotiated passes at an altitude of over 2,000 meters (6,600 feet) and traversed the boundless expanse of the prairie, passed through four time zones, spent the night in gravel pits, on lakeshores, in thick forests and on the open prairie, while often enough the rumbling of our van continued to invade our dreams. Now our first major goal has been achieved, and we can smile with some pride – and relief. Time for a few days' break.

We spend them in Fairbanks. At Rivers Edge Campground we stake out a position on the riverbank and encounter a dyed-in-the-wool traveling community. South Tyrolean Thomas is cycling through Alaska on a recumbent bicycle, Munich native Roland is on the road in an old Volkswagen bus with built-in wood-burning stove, Californians Lehel and Laura are driving a 1968 Unimog, Gene and Gayl from Wisconsin have a spacious RV, while Dutch couple Haye and Willeke boast a rusted Land Cruiser.

Left: Definitely worth a look – signpost forest in Watson Lake, Yukon, started by soldier Carl K. Lindley in 1942. Bottom left: Trucker in Fairbanks, Alaska.

In the evenings we sit together in varying groups, eating freshly caught fish from the river and swapping experiences and tips. In the short nights – daybreak is a mere three hours after sundown – the roar of our diesel engine gradually ebbs in our ears.

A mere 200 kilometers (120 miles) or so south-east of Fairbanks is Denali National Park, and at its center the "mountain of mountains," Mount McKinley. At 6,194 meters (20,316 feet), it's the highest mountain in North America. Although named after former US President William McKinley, it's known by everyone here as "Denali," a Native American word meaning "the high one," so we adopt the name too. Statistics show that at the height of summer Denali is only visible one day in three; for the rest of the time the view of the peak is obscured by clouds. We attentively follow the weather reports on the Web, and when blue skies are forecast for the next few days we set off. Not without reserving tickets in advance for the shuttle bus, for which reservations and payment are compulsory; entering the National Park by car is not permitted. A pity, but it makes sense: sixty buses, each carrying an average of thirty passengers, drive through the park daily. Imagine these throngs in private vehicles – no bears would ever show their faces at Denali again. So two days later we find ourselves sitting in a converted school bus and approaching the mountain silhouetted against a cloudless sky. We pass through barren tundra which gradually merges into even more barren grassy steppes. It's wild, big country here, and it's pretty close to the image of Alaska I still remember from my childhood reading of Jack London.

A stop sign as target ...!

*Above: The ultimate mountain – Mount McKinley in Denali National Park. Right: The bald eagle, the symbol and national bird of the USA.*

On the first few kilometers of our trip we see caribou – the North American relatives of Northern European reindeer – in the valley, grazing among the undergrowth of the tundra. We spot a moose in the distance and, shortly afterwards, our first grizzly; a solitary male ambles past us along a hill crest, moving rapidly and even lightly despite its enormous body weight of up to 400 kilos. Just a few kilometers further on we watch a mother grizzly with triplets taking a bath in a pool, then another family of three hunting a squirrel.

That's eight grizzlies in four hours. We feel as if we're in a "National Geographic" movie where the main hero has been sidelined into a bit part; Denali rises snow-covered and majestic from the pale yellow grass of the steppes. The difference in altitude between Wonder Lake, next to which we have a simple picnic, and the summit of Denali is 5,500 meters (18,040 feet). Such precipitous escarpments can't even be found in the Himalayas!

The distance between raw wilderness and rough-hewn city life is an asphalt road of scarce-

ly 350 kilometers (210 miles). In Anchorage, the largest city in Alaska, a ferocious manner is prized as a virtue. America's reputation for friendly service, so often and so rightly praised, seems to have been frozen in polar shock. I visit a hairdresser in a shopping mall. I have an appointment at twelve, stroll in just before twelve, and am outside again at – I swear – nine minutes past twelve, twenty-eight dollars lighter and with a few chunks hacked off my otherwise untouched hair. Of course I could have insisted on a little more enthusiasm, but who knows what

havoc the lady with the grim expression could have wreaked with her scissors! Nevertheless, we stay a further three nights; Lucy has her second service. Let's hope the mechanic is more motivated.

The Kenai Peninsula to the south of Anchorage is a jewel of creation! Along the Sterling Highway at the heart of the peninsula we pass crystal-clear lakes and rivers. At Russian River, shortly before its confluence with Kenai River, we turn into a dead-end road which brings us, after 3 kilometers (2 miles), to a sim-

ple campground in a forest clearing. We swiftly set up camp, fetch kindling for the evening and grab camera and fishing-rod. Walking the few hundred meters (a few hundred feet) through the wood to the river, we encounter a fascinating natural spectacle: the crystalline water is boiling with hundreds of bright red salmon toiling against the current. Here, at the place of their birth, they spawn and die. The river washes countless dead and dying fish into the valley. What a sad, beautiful story of life, death and re-birth.

We follow the next bend of the river in search of a sunny spot and suddenly stop in our tracks, stunned. Two grizzly bears are standing scarcely 20 meters (66 feet) ahead of us. We've read so much about unexpected encounters with these dangerous animals – now it's time to put our reading to the test. We stand calmly, making our presence known by speaking and gesturing with our arms. One of the grizzlies is standing on the opposite bank devouring a

Species preservation at any cost

Facing page, top:
Glacier at Seward on the Kenai peninsula.
Bottom left: Grizzly bear at Russian River.

# Dalton Highway

Although seven times larger than Germany, Alaska has only around 250,000 inhabitants, more than half of whom live near the two largest cities in the state: Anchorage and Fairbanks. The rest of the vast country is almost uninhabited. Its boundless space and untamed natural landscape do not reveal themselves along the developed roads where gas stations, campgrounds and even drive-in espresso joints succeed each other at convenient intervals. To approach the wild, primordial land, we have to leave the asphalt road behind.

Taking Dalton Highway, we plan to cross the Arctic Circle and traverse the desolate tundra to the Arctic Ocean in Alaska's far north. This highway runs alongside the Trans-Alaska Pipeline and was primarily designed as a supply route for the oilfields in Prudhoe Bay. However, "highway" is too flattering a term for these 600 kilometers (360 miles) of rough, often stony track, where the longest section without any possibility of buying provisions (between Coldfoot and Deadhorse) is 368 kilometers (221 miles) long. Imagine the route between Munich and Frankfurt without a gas station or emergency telephone. We have to calculate our gas reserves accordingly. There is no possibility of buying groceries along Dalton Highway, so we stock up on provisions for our eight-day drive.

Another 240 miles = 384 kilometers (230 miles) to go

According to "The Milepost", the bible of all Alaska travelers, the first few kilometers (miles) outside Livengood are harmless. And we actually find ourselves driving along a halfway decent road. But because of the dry summer, extensive areas of the forest here are on fire and the smoke hampers visibility enormously; at some points we can see no further than 200 meters (656 feet) ahead. Only after 90 kilometers (54 miles), to the north of the Yukon River, does the air clear to reveal fields of lilac fireweed, the first plant to grow on the scorched earth left by forest fires. We travel through mountainous countryside and watch out for bears, moose and caribou. But the oil pipeline alongside the road doesn't fit the picture, and distracts us for the whole journey as a constant reminder that humankind has taken over the whole of the planet, for its own purposes. Occasionally a heavy truck approaches from the other direction. When this happens, the required procedure is to brake sharply, move as far over to the right as the track will allow and send up a prayer that the windshield will hold. Which, by the way, it doesn't. We collect a couple of trophies in the shape of a 30-centimeter (11.70 inches) crack on the driver's side and two impact points on the right. Our first night is spent on a hillock in the midst of this primal country, surrounded by the wild northern landscape scarred by the pipeline and illuminated by the never-ending sunset. Darkness does not fall until around midnight, and soon afterwards the dawn rises in the east. In the brief night hours we keep watch for the Northern Lights, but there is no sign of the colorful natural phenomenon. Yet when we turn our backs on the pipeline and gaze into the distance, we gradually begin to recognize Alaska's true magic.

The next day we cross the Arctic Circle, leaving the tree line behind us and heading for the barren tundra where not even scrub grows, but only moss, lichen and grasses. The region is under permafrost; the earth is permanently frozen all year round. Even the warm summer weather – our thermometer shows an impressive 18 degrees – is no more than a superficial challenge to the permafrost. The ice remains under a thin layer of thawed earth, preventing rain and melt water from soaking into the ground and forming countless pools and lakes. At one of these lakes we unpack the canoe from the roof and paddle off – but our trip is short: at the next but one curve the lake narrows to a tiny stream, and we're forced to turn back. And yet here, away from the road and the pipeline,

A rough and rocky ride – Dalton Highway

metaphor; a depressing conglomeration of corrugated iron huts, trucks and oil barrels (but no dead horses) make up the USA's most northerly outpost, plus a gigantic oil well somewhat further towards the polar sea, only attainable by people who slide hard cash over the oil-smeared counter for a guided tour. But the weather is dreadful, temperatures plummeting from sixteen to eight degrees within a few kilometers (miles), and the town is shrouded in clouds while 30 kilometers (18 miles) further south the sun is

there is a stillness and isolation that is palpable, that can be felt with all the senses. Lucy toils up stony, steep tracks to Atigun Pass. In first gear our speed is scarcely faster than walking pace. The diesel truck coughs as it drags its four tons up the gradient, breaking into a sweat. The temperature indicator swings alarmingly to the right – reminding us of a gearbox failure in Norway after a steep climb to a mountain pass, also above the Arctic Circle. But Lucy pulls through bravely. When we reach the summit, all three of us draw deep breaths.

On the other side of the mountain, we race down into the valley and spend the night at Galbraith Lake, teeming with fish. Others have told us that fishing here is child's play. But I have an aura which every fish on the planet seems to scent, and which drives them to take flight in panic. I stand in the water until twilight (an angler's license in my pocket which cost me 50 dollars) but have no success. No barbecued fresh fish tonight then, but a scrumptious vegetable stir-fry prepared by Sabine. Also delicious!

The next day we reach Deadhorse on Prudhoe Bay, the end of Dalton Highway. The name is evidently a

shining. Despite this, Deadhorse deserves a heavily underlined entry in our diary as the most northerly point of our journey and, in a way, the starting-point of our actual plan itself. There are no roads, at least no public roads, which could take us further north to the polar sea. From now on, we will travel south until, in around twenty months, another ocean – this time the Antarctic – will again prevent us from going any farther. This makes us pause for a while. Our mood wavers between enthusiastic confidence and silent trepidation. Will we ever reach Tierra del Fuego?

We leave Deadhorse the same evening. There is nothing to keep us here save a barrel of diesel, which we leave 160 liters lighter, and a tiny store in which we buy the most popular souvenir of the otherwise desolate hamlet: a sticker which reads "A rough & rocky ride: JAMES DALTON HIGHWAY; Livengood to Deadhorse". Three days later we're back in Fairbanks, our sticker clearly visible on the door to our living area, and we're reveling in electricity, hot showers, flushing toilets, wireless access and … fresh fish from the supermarket!

salmon, while the other is sitting in the water and seems to be waiting for its dinner to be washed into its mighty claws of its own accord. Both are young animals, not yet fully grown. They spot us – a critical moment. If grizzlies feel surprised or threatened, they occasionally become aggressive and attack human beings. There's no point in running away – brown bears can run up to 55 kilometers per hour (33 miles). While black bears may be scared off by stout blows of the fist and loud shouting, brown bears are unimpressed by such measures; they have no natural enemies. The most effective method of repelling brown bears is a special anti-bear spray, good-quality brands of which cost around forty dollars in specialist stores. Ours is in the toolbox back at camp. The grizzlies look up and stare at us. They watch us for a while and … then lose all interest. Sabine wants us to withdraw warily, but a few photos are essential. I slowly crouch down and take the camera out of the bag, change the lens, check the viewfinder and press the shutter. The bear in the water hears the sound and looks up again, mustering me with a nonchalant air that indicates his superiority and seems to say, "This is my world, and you, human, are only tolerated as a guest!"

The bear returns to his dinner, looking almost cute as he does so, and I rapidly shoot twenty or thirty photos before we slowly retreat, walking backwards. A few hundred meters downriver, we stand stock-still on the bank and stare at each other, speechless. What an incredible encounter with nature! And it's something that anyone in danger of becoming too self-important should experience. In a fraction of a second, it readjusts our perspectives and opens our eyes to a feeling which we have left all too far behind us: humility.

The Alaskan coast has a wild beauty. Rough waves break against several thousand islands and rocky islets which provide refuge for countless waterfowl, many of them endangered species. Rare types of albatross, cormorant, gull and guillemot settle in the virgin natural habitat off the coast, while mighty bald eagles nest inland. In sleepy Seward we take a boat for a ten-hour tour to explore the windswept coastal

Left page, top: Homer on the furthest top of the Kenai peninsula. Bottom: Fascinating boat trips depart from Seward harbor. Left: The people reflect the country.

world at close quarters. We glide past calving glaciers, watch otters and sea-lions and spot a colony of whales in the distance. The air is chill, the waves lash, the wind blusters across the deck – a dramatic scene that sears itself into our memories.

Our next stop is Haines, where we board a ferry for a three-day cruise along the Inside Passage, away from the wilderness and back to British Columbia and Canada. By now it is early September, and the first frosty nights announce the impending arrival of the long winter. The day before we leave, snow falls higher up the mountains, the campgrounds close, and the lights in Alaska go out – literally. The many grandiose experiences of nature we've enjoyed, make leaving this magnificent wonderland difficult to bear. Will we ever see the region again, its barren tundra, its endless forests, its snow-covered peaks, its tossing ocean? We vow to return. We'll never forget Alaska.

Extremely rare sea otters

# The West Coast: Land of Boundless Freedom

"The road is life."

Jack Kerouac

[km/miles 14,534/8,720 to 18,923/11,354|
Haines – San Francisco]

Back in urban life: Vancouver in British Columbia.

The ferry deposits us on US soil; we disembark in the little town of Bellingham, just the other side of the Canadian border. Coming from the rugged Alaskan wilderness into the commercialization of America's West Coast is like being catapulted into a new galaxy. We're in no hurry to move south, so we turn around and head in the opposite direction, crossing the Canadian border once again and approaching Vancouver, the capital of British Columbia.

After our weeks of secluded isolation, we dizzily plunge into the glitter of the big city, finding a centrally located hotel room, investigating the city, Gastown and Chinatown on foot – and returning to our hotel hours later, exhausted and sobered. It was all too much of a good thing; the enticing shopping malls, the roar of the traffic in the streets, and above all the countless junkies in and around Chinatown – even in front of our hotel – all prompt us to leave Vancouver as fast as possible. We sense that we are being unfair to the city. Perhaps we should have accustomed ourselves more cautiously to its bustle, perhaps we should have taken a hotel in a quieter district and might then have seen Vancouver from a different perspective – but as it is, we are drawn out of the city and back to the wild. We treat ourselves to an elegant dinner in the "Top of Vancouver" revolving restaurant in Harbour Tower and drink in the panorama of the city's sea of lights; but

the next day we check out of our hotel and once again board a ship for the two-hour trip to Vancouver Island.

At just under 32,000 square kilometers (12,160 square miles), Vancouver Island is the largest Pacific island in North America, somewhat smaller than the state of Baden-Württemberg in Germany and, with over 500,000 inhabitants, similarly densely populated. However, the majority of the island-dwellers live along the milder and more protected east and south coasts, while the west coast on the open North Pacific is sparsely settled, wild and rugged – the perfect territory for us! From Nanaimo we head west along the narrow, twisting Highway 4 towards the Pacific Rim National Park.

We strike camp at Ucluelet, a former fishing village, and use it as a base from which to explore the island's west coast, speeding out into the Pacific in a Zodiac boat for a short whale-watching tour. The weather is terrible and whales are few and far between. We imagine we can make out the blurred silhouettes of an orca and two gray whales through the dense veil of rain, and the coastline is home to whole colonies of sea-lions. A few miles further north up the coast towards Tofino, areas of rainforest still survive; we take the opportunity to explore them. These primeval landscapes are an all-round experience for the senses; surrounded by a cornucopia of lush, rich shades of green, you

inhale the scent of dark, moldering earth, hear the rippling of watercourses, the rustle of leaves, the creaking of ancient trees; you taste the sweet moistness of the air and your sixth sense informs you that gnomes and elves are hiding behind the thick leaves and observing your every step. We adore these murky, magical worlds of light and shade, hidden paths and mysterious crannies that generate a wonderful condition of childlike excitement in us. We conclude our stay on Vancouver Island with a two-day canoe tour of the fjord-like channels around Tofino before bidding a final farewell to Canada, a land we have truly come to love in the past weeks for the wildness of its nature and, even more so, for its friendly, mellow people. Canada could really be a country to become attached to. We add it to our "We could live here" list (if only the winters there weren't so darned long …).

We leave the island on a ferry, a two-hour trip which takes us to Anacortes on US soil. From here we speed to Seattle, sixty miles away, and spend a pleasant if unspectacular day there visiting the Seattle Aquarium and strolling through attractive Pike Place Market, where fish, vegetables and crafts are sold under arcades;

*Above: Rough seas on Oregon's west coast. Left: We can be sure of a sympathetic glance – Harley rider in Sonoma Valley.*

# Wilderness, Winds and Witticisms

The narrow Highway No. 4 twists endlessly through the dense forests in the west of Vancouver Island. We turn right shortly before the deep gray waters of Kennedy Lake, and follow a bumpy track muddy from the rain of the last few days and even flooded in places – not easy to drive. After 18 kilometers (11 miles) the track ends at the clear waters of Torquat Bay. The bay curves into the land in a broad arc, narrowing into a slim, fjord-like finger at its western edge.

We park Lucy at a little campground on the banks, take down the canoe, pack sleeping-bags, tent, mats, provisions and drinking water and paddle off. We're lucky with the weather; the sun shines from a cloudless sky and paints the surroundings in glowing colors. Verdant slopes rise to our right and left. At first we paddle through open water, far from the bank, making good progress with rhythmic, effortless strokes and soon reaching the narrow inlet of Torquat Bay. From here, we stay close to the banks.

No houses perch on the slopes, no roads – not even a path – lead through the dense undergrowth to the water. Wilderness and nothing but wilderness surrounds us on all sides. We watch sea lions and otters in the water, and in a clearing on the banks a black bear ambles across the scree scarcely 5 meters (16 feet) away from us. We land on a little islet with a flat, stony beach and bathe in the chilly water. Craggy rock formations near the shore are thickly festooned with oysters. We harvest some with our pocket-knife, open them and eat them raw – delicious! – before moving on. The GPS mounted on the front of the canoe reliably charts our position at all times.

After five hours our arms gradually grow tired, the sun is level with the water and it's time to find a spot for the night. We set up camp on a narrow spit of land, pitch the tent and collect wood for a fire over which we later plan to fix spaghetti, opening a jar of pesto as a start. The sun has now set and a glittering ceiling of stars unfurls above us. The black water slowly retreats, the tide uncovering a

Thawing out!

stretch of scree strewn with starfish and oysters – these are magical moments. Yet during the night we both sleep uneasily, nervously listening to the noises around us – rustlings, splashing and cracking – let's hope a bear doesn't stumble across our tent...! Sleep evades us until the early hours of the morning.

Our breakfast at sunrise consists of muesli bars and tea. We are soon ready to set off down yesterday's route, this time heading for the opposite bank. But today requires far more effort as the wind and tide work against us.

A gale blows around our heads, and black rain clouds tower in the distance. Arms weary, we reach the last but most difficult section – the open water, where high waves are hammering against the cliffs. Our canoe is not designed for these conditions, we are extremely inexperienced and our muscles are exhausted. For long stretches we have the feeling that we are making no progress against the wind and waves, and the shore that is our destination is far, far away. Water sloshes over the edge of the canoe, and we sit in the chilly wetness as feelings of nervousness mount! To distract ourselves we tell each other jokes. Although neither of us feels like laughing, it helps somehow; just when neither of us can think of another joke to save our lives, we finally reach land. It is afternoon. Completely Exhausted, we drag the canoe up the shore, crawl into our berth and snooze for a while!

A few hours later the clouds have vanished, the wind has dropped and our nerves are calmer. We pack up our belongings and spend the evening in Lucy over a bottle of red wine, listening to Chet Baker and gazing at each other, grinning. What an adventure, we now think, content and relieved in our safe haven. Okay, maybe the next time we'll pay more attention to the weather report, and… maybe as greenhorns we should stay away from open waters. A Persian proverb advises that "The best thing to bring home from a journey is your safe skin". True enough, but the second best thing is a fund of thrilling stories!

we find a wonderful little restaurant purely by chance on the first floor of an old townhouse, where we sit at a long bar, order a light lunch and enjoy the ambitious cuisine. Seattle is hip in the US, the high-tech capital and a hotbed of trends in music and fashion. And yet after a day's sightseeing, we leave the metropolis of the north-west – we're just not in the mood for cities.

From then on, we follow the North Pacific coast of Washington and Oregon through a wilderness that unfurls majestically before us; craggy, forested foothills, mighty volcanic craters, beaches of fine sand where the primordial power of the mighty ocean crashes down – a playground of creation. Highway 101 in Oregon is regarded as one of the most beautiful coastal roads in North America. In an astonishingly wise, very un-American piece of foresight, a regulation was passed that beaches cannot be privately owned and must be open to the pub-

lic. As a result, today the coast of Oregon is completely free from hotels, unspoilt and gloriously wild. However, the weather at this time is no less wild, with mist and rain often obscuring any view of the ocean. We continually put on rain gear and trek along isolated beaches, but often the rough sea vanishes behind an impenetrable wall of lashing rain. Finally, we flee to the hinterland. At Crater Lake in the National Park of the same name, we circle a deep blue lake 11 kilometers (6.5 miles) in diameter. When Mount Mazama erupted 6,800 years ago, the peak collapsed inward to form this perfectly symmetrical crater. At an altitude of over 2,000 meters (6,560 feet), it's cold up here, surrounded by remnants of snow from a storm a few days ago. Fall is nipping at our heels. The little town of Ashland, close to the Californian border, is regarded as southern Oregon's cultural center. It's the home of the

*Relic of the pre-cell age*

*Above: Sea-lion colony in Pacific Rim National Park, Vancouver Island.*

Above: Columns of the earth – Redwoods in California.
Right: Nature sets the record straight on the highway in Prairie Creek Redwood State Park.

Oregon Shakespeare Festival, the fame of which extends beyond the national borders. Shakespearean and contemporary dramas are performed on three stages, one outdoors, between February and October. Tickets for the classics are sold out months in advance. We manage to find two for the 1930s play "Room Service" by John Murray and Allen Boretz. But what was advertised as an "homage to American theater" proves to be no more than a clichéd screwball comedy and we are driven to leave after the first act. Ashland itself, however, is worth a visit. The main street is lined with restaurants, delicatessens, galleries, antique stores and fashion boutiques; the city park (Lithia Park) extends up the hill through fall foliage and beyond the town boundaries. We pamper ourselves a little, and Lucy also gets a treat: her well-earned third service.

"Many Americans believe that they haven't achieved their life's goal until they are finally living in California, the land of boundless free-

scenery. These are the last redwood forests, which once covered California's entire coastal mountains. Redwoods (sequoia) are believed to be the world's tallest plants: they can grow to over 100 meters (328 feet) high and reach ages of up to 2,000 years.

In Prairie Creek Redwood State Park, we park Lucy at the edge of the forest, pack a picnic, water and rain gear into a rucksack and hike into forests that are absolutely unique. The trees soar into the sky like classical columns, their smooth trunks fanning out into a mighty crown far, far above and joining to form a magnificent vaulted roof that gives shelter to complex biotopes. Hosts of plants, including young redwoods, grow in the soil that accumulates on their branches. The crown of a single tree in State Park was found to have 148 branches, which themselves can grow to enormous dimensions at these heights, in turn creating new habitats for plants and even animals which never touch the earth we walk upon. Another rich-

*Above: Brilliant fall sunshine over Sonoma Valley wine country. Left: Merlot or Cabernet? Wine-tasting in California.*

dom…" we read in a magazine, and the Lonely Planet guide opens with the words: "… California will provide you with dreams enough for a lifetime!" Wow! This awakens expectations clamoring to be fulfilled. The weather, however, fails to measure up to the dream, and there's no sign of surfing beauties or bikini belles far and wide! Instead, just to the south of the border we enter an area of almost unreal natural

*San Francisco, high up on our "We could live here" list.*

ly diverse forest thus develops 50 meters (164 feet) above the ground – a new generation borne on the shoulders of its own ancestors. If there really is a Creator, he certainly produced a magnificent masterpiece in these forests. We spend the whole day there, clambering up narrow paths to the top of steep cliffs, splashing through crystal streams in broad valleys and listening to the Pacific waves thunder in the distance. A world evolved here over the course of millennia, a world which European settlers, with their "godly" mission to subjugate the earth, managed to wipe out almost completely in less than two hundred years. Only four percent of the original redwood forests are still in existence!

While the forests of Northern California reveal the destructive nature of humankind, a few hundred kilometers (miles) to the south we shown to be an equally creative and sensuous species. We arrive at Sonoma Valley, Califor-

nia's wine-growing country north of San Francisco, and set up a base camp at a shady campground amid the pretty vineyards. We revive our little scooter (earning many a pitying glance from a Harley rider in the process) and spend the next two days of sunshine traveling from winery to winery and tasting our way from north to south. The main varieties grown here are Zinfandel, Chardonnay and Traminer, which develop rich fruit and body in the favorable climate. American wine may have a doubtful reputation because of the wood chips and artificial flavorings which are permitted additives over here, but … it tastes great!

We finally arrive in San Francisco, falling for the city's manifest charm as soon as we drive into it. Its forty and more hills are lined with Victorian houses, it is surrounded by water on three sides, and the Golden Gate Bridge is rightly considered the world's most beautiful bridge. Around 800,000 highly individual people live

here, pursuing a vibrant culture that has brought so much creative energy into the world: beat, hippies, Flower Power, Peace and Love, heterosexual – and later homosexual – revolution were all movements that originated here. According to a magazine we read, "San Francisco has always attracted outsiders, as one of the few places where freaks are rewarded and where being normal is abnormal." On foot and by cablecar, a mode of transport as delightful as it is antiquated, we explore Chinatown, North Beach, Russian Hill and Haight Ashbury, the birthplace of the Summer of Love; we visit the San Francisco Museum of Modern Art and the outstanding Asian Art Museum; we breakfast in the coffee shop on the corner and linger in tiny restaurants on Fisherman's Wharf, overflowing with kitsch and fellow patrons, until long into the night. After only a short time we no longer feel like outside observers but become part of this gloriously colorful multicultural society. When we move on after four days, another name has appeared on our "We could live here" list – hardly surprising. Heavens, the list is growing so fast here in the western USA. We may have to apply tougher criteria for inclusion …!

Delightfully antiquated ...

43

# Crossing the Sierra Nevada: Abyss

*"It's not about what you see, but how you see it."*
*Anselm Adams, photographer*

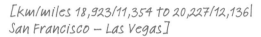

[km/miles 18,923/11,354 to 20,227/12,136|
San Francisco – Las Vegas]

*Right page: Fall in the Sierra Nevada Facing page: Merced River in Yosemite National Park.*

From San Francisco we head east down the curves of Highway 120 as it gently snakes from sea level up to the Sierra Nevada mountains over 2,000 meters (6,560 feet) higher. Though our stay in the big city was pleasant, it's good to be on the road again, driving down the highway and watching the green countryside rolling past our window. And though we enjoyed our nights in the hotel, we're equally happy to exchange our spacious room there for Lucy's cramped living quarters. The best place to sleep is under our own coverlet in the alcove above the cab, 1.90 meters (6 feet) above our surroundings of lush meadow, damp forest or dusty desert.

300 kilometers (180 miles) east of San Francisco we park Lucy at a lookout point, stroll over to the edge and gaze down into a valley which legendary American pioneer John Muir is said to have described as "the grandest of all special temples of Nature": the Yosemite Valley.

According to the brochure, the Native Americans named this place "Ahwahnee," meaning "a mouth open in astonishment." Yosemite Valley was created in the last million years by glacial erosion. Only 13 kilometers (8 miles) long and a mere 1,600 meters (5,248 feet) wide, the valley has spectacular granite walls, at some points soaring almost sheer to heights of 1,000 meters (2,380 feet) on both sides, which make our jaws drop.

We cautiously coast down a steep track of switchbacks into the valley, where the road fol-

lows the Merced River through a scene of placid beauty: lush green meadows, gurgling streams and dark mountain forests. Attracting over 3.5 million visitors every year, Yosemite National Park is one of the most popular destinations in America. Some souls we encountered on our travels advised us to avoid the park because of the crowds – and thank heavens we ignored them. Now, at the end of October, the stream of tourists has reached a bearable level. We find a nice corner for Lucy in the campground and set up for a three-night stay.

In the next few days we hike through a nature park positively exploding with fall colors. We roam forests of giant sequoias over one 100 meters (328 feet) high, up to 3,000 years old and weighing 6,000 tons. We clamber over worn granite steps to craggy summits over which countless waterfalls pour into the valley below. The largest, Yosemite Falls, is 739 meters (2,424 feet) high. But at this time of year, only a trickle splashes over the cliffs – unlike Vernal Fall, which thunders into the depths with magnificently profligate force. In the evening we sit around a camp fire in a forest clearing, the bare cliffs rising around us. It's cold even here in the valley; winter has long reached the heights. A hungry coyote slinks cautiously past, and later a mother black bear strolls through the camp with her cub. In the night we hear the fall wind in the rustling leaves, howling coyotes in the distance – and our neighbor snoring in the next

tent. Ah, the sounds of the wild! At Tioga Pass to the north of the valley, we climb to altitudes of over 3,000 meters (9,840 feet). At 2,000 meters (6,560 feet) Lucy belches forth impressive clouds of black smoke, at 2,500 meters (8,200 feet) her engine begins to make loud knocking sounds, and at 3,000 meters (9,840 feet) she is reduced to tormented gasping. At the top we find icy temperatures but brilliant sunshine, and ramble over snowy meadows along narrow streams. We later hear that the night after our stroll brought violent snowstorms and the pass was closed the next morning, remaining so until the following May. We are the very last to cross Tioga Pass this year.

On the eastern slopes of the Sierra Nevada the scenery changes dramatically within the space of only a few kilometers (miles). First immersed in vibrant fall colors, we now enter barren bush country. Once again we climb up to a pass at an altitude of 2,000 meters (6,560 feet) before the road plummets down into Death Valley, 80 meters (262 feet) below sea level. Yester-

day we stood at the torrents of Vernal Fall thundering into the depths; today we're in the middle of the desert! Death Valley is North America's hottest, driest and lowest-lying region, a broad valley enclosed by a rampart of mountains which few rain clouds succeed in crossing. Its barren landscape is made up of rock, scree, sparse, flat scrub, a few sand dunes and salt lakes. We're transfixed. We love deserts, and have had our most powerful travel experiences there; here, too, a state of mind develops that – like all forms of love – is as irrational as it is indescribable. It seems as if the more austere and rudimentary our surroundings are, the closer we come to approaching our true selves. Where there is nothing but empty, broad landscape and infinite, cloudless sky, no obstacles obscure our view of essentials, our encounter with our inner selves. It is in deserts or desert-like landscapes that we undergo our most intense experiences of ourselves and of traveling; in Alaska's treeless tundra, in the dunes of Australia's Simpson Desert, in the northern Sahara, and once again

here in Death Valley, where we spend three days and nights. At this time of year daytime temperatures reach a pleasant twenty degrees Celsius, and the nights are surprisingly mild. We hike through jagged canyons and elongated sand dunes, encountering a host of eccentrics along the way. Take Laura-Belle and Bob for example, a delightful senior couple in a scarcely less senior pick-up. They've driven from Bishop, 200 kilometers (120 miles) away, to spend a day at the pool at Stovepipe Well. The entrance charge is 2.50 dollars for a whole day – cheaper than any pools at home, they inform us.

Laura-Bell, Bob and Sabine

Leaving Death Valley behind us, we again plunge into the depths – but this time they're moral, not geographical. In less than three hours the glittering world of Las Vegas rears up before us – like a different planet after our powerful experiences of nature in the past few days! The heart of the arid Mojave Desert is home to the

Right: Sand dunes in Death Valley. Opposite page, top and bottom: Magnificent fake – Las Vegas in all its glitter and glamour.

Salt lake in Death Valley

greatest conglomeration of casinos, showrooms, bordellos and fake plaster stage sets imaginable. The world-famous boulevard "The Strip" is lined with gigantic casino hotels, each outdoing the other in their overblown extravagance. Every half-hour the "Treasure Island" offers pirate shipwrecks while a volcano erupts in the "Mirage," the "Bellagio,"competes with a colossal show of "dancing waters," and in the "Venetian" gondoliers paddle along an artificial Canal Grande on the first floor of the shopping mall. Just to remind you: we're in a desert here!

We strive to maintain some show of decency and book into the "Aladin;" after all, the lavish interior does feature an Arabic theme which is slightly desert-related. Our room is enormous, the casino is vast and the attached shopping center in the style of a Moroccan souk is breathtaking. We "do" all the major theme hotels on the "Strip" (the scaled-down Eiffel Tower in "Paris – Las Vegas," the covered St. Mark's Square in the "Venetian," the South Sea beach in "Mandalay Bay," manhole covers exuding steam in the lobby of "New York - New York"),

we play poker on slot machines (putting in thirty dollars and winning eighty!), feast in "Treasure Island" on the best pasta we've had since leaving home almost six months ago, and our own "Aladin," a little café at a covered pool (which stages a thunderstorm every half-hour), serves such a superb espresso that it almost knocks me off my chair. We watch the Cirque du Soleil show "Mystère" at "Treasure Island," applauding enthusiastically, and spend evenings at the bar in "Paris - Las Vegas" sipping a cognac and waving away the waiter's offer of ice. Along the road back to our hotel, fat gamblers clutching half-full whiskey bottles stagger towards us and Latinos press stacks of picture cards for 35-dollar-an-hour prostitutes into our hands. Las Vegas focuses on every possible facet of immoderacy. It's fascinating and disgusting and spectacular and vulgar. It's magnificently immoral yet American through and through, a place that's as seductive as it's intolerable!

After three nights it's high time to drag ourselves away from the pull of this depraved and addictive place. Nursing respectable hangovers, we resume our route east, to a region of stupendous and totally authentic natural landscapes that show Las Vegas up as the monumental fake that it is – we're headed for Canyon Country!

Primeval landscape of sacred grandeur: Monument Valley

# Canyon Country: Forces of Nature at Play

"I am the land. My eyes are the sky. My limbs are the trees. I am the rock, the deep water. I am not here to dominate or exploit nature. I am nature myself."
*Saying of the Hopi Indians*

[km/miles 20,227/12,136 to 24,665/14,799]
Las Vegas – San Diego]

*Solitary tour outpost in the Arizona desert.*

We've arrived in a wondrous land of sculptures and monuments, of cliché and yearning. A land where nature goes wild. We climb the heights of the Colorado Plateau, an upland plain in the Four Corners region of the United States where Arizona, Utah, Colorado and New Mexico meet. Its vital statistics are arresting; the plateau covers an area of around 620,000 square kilometers (235,600 square miles), roughly the size of Germany and Italy together, and its average height above sea level is almost 2,000 meters (6,560 feet). With an annual rainfall of around 50 centimeters (19.5 inches), the Colorado Plateau region is classified as semi-arid. Sun, wind, water, ice and creeping destruction by vegetation have carved impressive gorges in the earth and shaped magnificent sandstone sculptures.

Our "Tour de Gorges" starts at Zion National Park in the south-western tip of Utah. Here, over the course of millennia, the Virgin River has sliced a deep canyon. Sheer cliffs of white, pink and rust-colored rock soar, while down at the river a picturesque world of plants and flowers flourishes in the season's fall colors; by contrast, the stony plateau is dominated by pallid, thorny scrub.

We explore the valley on our scooter and ride up a steep pass road, dismounting at the top to continue on foot. A narrow track along the steep slope leads to Canyon Overlook, a platform offering a panoramic view over the gorge. Below us, the road snakes through the narrow valley, the steep cliffs changing color minute by minute in the setting sun from dull orange to vibrant red, pastel magenta and finally dark gray.

When we finally return to our spot in the picturesque campground near the river, we're amazed. Parked next to us is a camper with Munich license plates. What a surprise! Like us, Silvia and Christoph have been traveling through North America for six months, following a route that's almost identical to ours. They too plan to reach Tierra del Fuego by next Christmas. We sit around the campfire until far into the night, pooling our reserves of food to dish up a lavish banquet, plundering our wine stocks and swapping stories. Our paths are likely to cross often in the future.

Around 160 kilometers (96 miles) further northeast, we arrive at Bryce Canyon – which is actually not a canyon at all. In fact, what we're standing in front of is a vast escarpment over 700 meters (2,296 feet) deep in places and extending for around 40 kilometers (24 miles). Erosion shaped its rock formations, fifty million years old, into bizarre columns and towers known as hoodoos. A weird place. The needles of rock stand straight as stone sculptures in this mighty amphitheater. Transfixed and shivering,

we gaze down into this alien world 2,300 meters (7,544 feet) below.

It's like being on another planet. If one of the towers were suddenly to disgorge little green men with bulging heads and saucer-like eyes – we'd hardly skip a beat …

We drive over 3,000-meter (9,840 feet) passes high to reach Arches National Park. It's another spot where natural forces have worked to create elaborate statues: the action of water, ice and extreme temperatures and the movement of buried salt beds have conspired to shape the rocks into arches, some of enormous dimensions. The largest, Landscape Arch, is around 30 meters (98 feet) high and spans an incredible 100 meters (328 feet). The most beautiful of all these rock curves is Delicate Arch. We hike through the dusty semi-desert for an hour, clambering up to barren summits and panting in the thin air. For the last 300 meters (984 feet), a steep rock wall rises vertically at our sides, blocking our view of the landscape: but at the top the wall opens unexpectedly to reveal a panorama of the perfect stage. On the brink of a sloping stone plateau polished to smooth

*Above: View from Canyon Overlook into the gorges below, in Zion National Park. Left: We were there – Monument Valley, Arizona.*

finish, a towering rock archway of otherworldly beauty glows in the late afternoon sun. In the background, the escarpment falls steeply away to the broad plain, while the snow-capped summits of the Manti-La Sal Mountains rise in the distance. The whole landscape is of such breathtaking beauty that we are stunned, seating ourselves on the bare rock and drinking in this moment for an age. During the vacation season the place is overrun with tourists, yet now, in early November, we are alone for the time being. We gaze down on this flawless scene, feeling the dry wind on our skin, hearing the carping "awk, awk" of a crow above us and sensing our own pulses. We are thankful to be part of a divine whole. But after half an hour our reverie is shattered by the arrival of a group of tourists who beleaguer Delicate Arch, opening cans of beer and soon kicking up so much noise that it sounds like the patio of the pub down in Moab. The rocks are indifferent. They already stood proud 100,000 years ago when homo sapi-

ens made his first appearance, and they will certainly survive him. We leave the group to their revelries and descend. Thick clouds pile up, later bringing lightning and our first rain in weeks. With little improvement in the weather on the next morning, we cancel our plans to hike to Devils Garden and head south again, hoping for warmer and drier weather.

On the border between Utah and Arizona we cross Navajo country, the largest Indian reservation in the USA. The ancestors of the Navajos and the Apaches didn't migrate to this area from Canada until the 15th century, and came into contact with the Spanish in the following century; but it wasn't until the arrival of the Anglo-Saxons in the 19th century that their land was gradually taken from them, culminating in their banishment to the reservation in 1868. Today the Navajo people numbers around 175,000 and is the largest Native American tribe, over half of whom live here on the reservation. However, few people are about on the

Left: Another spectacle of creation – Joshua Tree National Monument in California.
Left bottom: In the maw of Antelope Canyon, Arizona.

"Let's ride to Arizona and cleanse the sun itself"

highway, which leads through joyless towns with gas stations, scattered shanties and RVs on blocks. Rough wooden sales booths line the street – all deserted.

At the heart of Indian country is the primeval landscape of Monument Valley, dominated by mighty sandstone cliffs as smooth as ice. Although this spot is sacred to the Navajos, it is universally familiar from TV commercials, Western movies and coffee-table travel books. We bounce down the stony track to the valley and spend the afternoon exploring vast pillars of rock in the barren semi-desert. Our camp site for the night is like a royal box overlooking breathtaking scenery: we are perched at the cliff edge that plunges into the valley and are treated to a sunset as beautiful as a painting – executed with an abundance of color.

We continue on our southbound route. The Colorado Plateau gradually reaches heights of over 2,200 meters (7,216 feet); Lucy emits asthmatic clouds of smoke and loud knocking noises, and we also have difficulty catching our breath. But then there is little more than a bare tollbooth to prepare us for the wonder which awaits at the South Rim: we stand at the "most spectacular hole in the ground anywhere," the Grand Canyon!

A channel carved by the Colorado River, around 450 kilometers (270 miles) long ago,

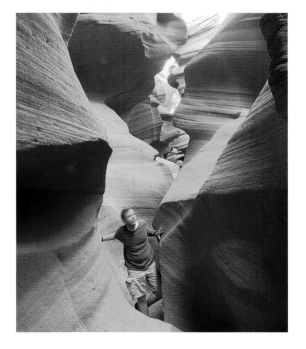

The bizarre sculptures in Bryce Canyon; like being on a different planet

*"Park Avenue" in Arches National Park*

16 kilometers (10 miles) wide and 1.6 kilometers (1 mile) deep. A vast underworld unfurls before us, a negative view of a mountain range, a "mysterious symbol of all landscapes," as Simone de Beauvoir described it. There may be canyons on this earth that are deeper or narrower, but there can be none more breathtaking. Dull yellow, copper, purple and smoky blue strata of rock pile upon each other while the evening sun pours its light over the canyon walls. We stand at the edge with a small cluster of other tourists from all over the world, as our gaze loses itself in this mighty gorge.

This region never stops delighting us. But as the saying goes, quit while the going's good. It's time to leave the United States. Our visas will expire soon, and we are gradually longing for warmer climes. In the last of our six nights at the Grand Canyon we experience temperatures of minus eleven and snow while the Web reports sunny twenty-one degrees for northern Ba-

ja California. Our months of travel through the United States have been as relaxed, as secure and smooth as our journey further south will be anything but.

We experienced magnificent scenery and incomparable natural spectacles. We encountered hospitable, warm and almost compulsively optimistic people, who frequently strove touchingly to portray their America in a better light than it was judged by outsiders at the time. We leave an America that is to be envied, despite its occasional sterility and excesses of commercialization, carrying a respectably lengthy "I could live here" list, to which we add one name at the end: Santa Fe in New Mexico! We feel so at home here that we have to persuade each other to continue our journey. But then we say to ourselves that if this spruced-up facsimile of the Latin world generates such enthusiasm in us, what must the original be like? So we're off … vamos a Mexico…!

# Descent into the Underworld

Two paths lead into the Grand Canyon, the mother of all canyons. At just under 15 kilometers (9 miles), the "Bright Angel" trail is longer but less steep, while the "South Kaibab" trail on which we will descend is far shorter at eleven kilometers (7 miles), but considerably steeper. In addition, no drinking water is available along the route. There is a difference in altitude of around 1,500 meters (4,920 feet) between the upper edge of the Canyon and the Colorado River below. The day before our descent we obtain a back country permit allowing us to walk the trail, and pack sleeping-bags, tent, provisions and water reserves in our rucksacks before going to bed early. The night is frosty, but Lucy is well insulated. The next day we march off in sunshine but icy temperatures.

The descent is steep, but not really difficult. An impressive landscape extends around us, with magnificent views. Only here can we develop a feel for the canyon's true dimensions, where the walls tower above us and the abyss yawns below. At this time of year few people are abroad on the narrow path; a caravan of six mules led by two rangers meet us half-way. The animals are laden with sacks – heaven only knows what's in them. After four hours we reach the Colorado, where the air is considerably milder. At the river we take off our shoes and socks and paddle in the cooling waters, which have taken 6.9 million years to slice their way through to this point. We pitch the tent at a designated campground, eat in the "Phantom Ranch" mountain canteen and are in our sleeping-bags by eight.

Our alarm clock rings at half-past six. It's still pitch-dark outside. We don our headlamps to give us enough light to pack up, eat a muesli bar, fill up all our water bottles and just as the first fingers of dawn can be seen in the east, set off for the long trek up the Bright Angel trail. We've read that eight to twelve hours are necessary to ascend, and since the sun sets at five we need to stick to our timetable unless we want to tackle the last kilometers in the dark. Statistically speaking, a rescue team is called out every two days to save someone who hasn't made it. The canyon claims its toll of victims every year.

At the same time as we set off, a group of six private schoolboys aged sixteen or so and their teacher start with us, storming off ahead. Oh, to be younger! The first few kilometers slope gradually up alongside the river, until the path turns off into a side gorge and steepens. We take a break for a "second breakfast" after only an hour. Before resuming the ascent we take out our alpenstocks, which prove to be an enormous help. At some point we overtake the school group and are flushed with pride – until the group overtakes us in turn and speeds ahead. A while later we catch up with them again, and so it continues as a pleasant camaraderie develops between us – as if we were spurring each other on. Halfway up at the "Indian Gardens," a lush oasis in the barren, rocky surroundings, we find drinking water and an earth closet. We feel every bone, but the worst section is still ahead of us.

The goal is downwards ...

The sneakiest thing about the Bright Angel trail is that the last third is far and away the toughest section of the whole route. Not only because the track is at its steepest; the air becomes thinner, making every movement tiring. By now the schoolboys have a head start on us. Our steps begin to drag, our drink breaks are closer and closer together, and still the rim seems to be an age away. We toil along meter by meter, by now marching to our own personal rhythm and neither of us inclined to talk. Instead, strange and unaccustomed thoughts surface in our minds: where have I come from? Where am I going? Where is the center of life? And ... er ... what exactly am I doing here?

We climb and climb. The final kilometer seems to stretch endlessly. Then we're at the top, and receive an uproarious welcome as the six schoolboys, their girlfriends who had stayed at the rim, and their teacher break into loud applause. We march through a guard of honor of cheering youngsters shouting: "Yeah, you did it!!" Falling into each other's arms, we feel pride and relief. And those sore muscles? Phooey! We'll endure them over the next few days with lofty equanimity.

San Diego
Tijuana
USA
Ciudad Juárez
Chihuahua
RIO Grande
MEXICO
La Paz
Zacatecas
Mazatlán
Tampico
PAZIFIC OCEAN
San Miguel
de Allende
Mexiko
City
Acapulco
0        310 miles
0        500 km

# Mexico's North: A World of Sensuous Opposites

"Poor Mexico, so far from God and so near the United States."

Porfirio Díaz, President of Mexico from 1884 to 1911

[km/miles 24,665/14,799 to 30,129/18,077| San Diego – Mexico City]

*Proud and vibrant, Mexicans never miss an opportunity to praise their country.*

Tecate, the Mexican border, Friday, December 15, just before noon. The sun labors through a milky, dull sky, casting its wan light over the desiccated, barren country. We slowly coast up to the border post. An overweight, mustachioed border guard leans indifferently against the open barrier, huge dark patches of sweat staining his otherwise immaculately pressed uniform shirt. He waves. What does he want? Stop? Stop and show papers? I brake, but he only waves more vigorously. He wants us to drive on. Drive on? We hesitantly coast on and on and on ... and finally arrive in the town center.

No, that can't be all there is! We were prepared for a lengthy immigration process, had checked a host of travel guides to find out what we need to take note of, and Silvia and Christoph, who are ahead of us, also e-mailed us some final tips. And now here we are on Mexican territory and never even had to show our passports? We turn round, drive the 500 meters (1640 feet) back to the border post, stop at the barrier and get out of the car. Now things start moving. The border guard pants towards us and emphatically insists that I move the vehicle ("no parrrking herrre"). I try to explain to him in English interspersed with a few scraps of Spanish that we need entry and vehicle papers,

upon which he directs us to a low office building and repeats his command to move Lucy with added emphasis. Well, what do you know? In the immigration office we have to fill out a form, then cross the road to a small cashier's office to fork out a fee of twenty US dollars and cross the street back again to the office, where we receive a tourist visa for six months, then back across the street to a different office where we apply for a vehicle permit for Lucy which costs another twenty-seven US dollars ... after an hour we've completed the procedure, high-five each other and finally, armed with all the stamps we need, drive into ... Mexico!

We haven't been on the bumpy asphalt southbound highway for ten minutes before we're pulled over by a Mexican police patrol. A police officer appears at our window (he could be the brother of the border guard) and patronizingly gives us to understand that we've been driving too fast in a school zone. Of course we weren't. Lucy can't go too fast – she's not built for it. Anyway, over the last few kilometers we've been overtaken by half of Tecate! Why doesn't anyone stop them? We start a discussion (pretty laborious given the language barrier) and ask where the speed limit sign is, whereupon the policeman retorts brusquely that I'm welcome to

Above: In the central region of Baja California the landscape is dominated by giant cardón cacti.
Left: Mexican cuisine, a journey of discovery in itself – eating in Mulege.

get into his police car and he'll drive me to the location of the sign. To underline his authority, he also stops another passing police car, and now we have to take the matter up with three mustachioed policemen. Great! Our crime carries a penalty of 150 pesos, we're informed. We have to accompany them to the police station, on the other side of town. "OK", we say. "Let's go." The trio hadn't expected this at all. I start Lucy's engine and wait for one of them to drive ahead. The "guardian of the peace" still has my papers – all excellent copies. The moustache gang finally starts moving, while we bring up the rear. After a few hundred meters they stop again, hand back our "papers" and issue a stern warning to obey the law in future. Then they roar off. 5 kilometers (3 miles) into Mexico, and we've already made the acquaintance of some corrupt policemen trying to boost their petty cash with our dollars. We've seen through their game! They were taken aback by our readiness to follow them instead of merely wiping out the whole affair with a modest donation. A trick we won't forget!

But now let's get going! The peninsula of Baja California dangles from the end of the US

*The "Mexico Bus" at Malecón in La Paz, capital of Baja California.*

state of California like a thin tail, 1,300 kilometers (780 miles) from north to south and varying from 45 to 70 kilometers (27 to 42 miles) in width. Its northern part, through which we drive in the first few days, is bare, dry and pretty monotonous. The MEX 1, a narrow asphalt highway, first runs along the west coast before turning off into the mountainous hinterland at El Rosario. Traffic is sparse. Mexicans have a unique style of driving in which street signs have a purely decorative function. Overtaking is practiced wherever the road is wide enough, and if a bend or a blind hump happens to be in the way … so what. The few dusty towns we pass are not exactly attractive; the houses are unprepossessing, although the people are proud, friendly and cheerful despite their poverty. Whenever we can, we eat lunch in one of the countless little street restaurants or snack bars. Mexican food is a journey of discovery in itself, the fusion of two cuisines – American Indian

and Spanish/European. Refried beans, rice and spicy salsa (chili sauce) appear on our plates almost every day, served with every possible variation of tortillas and a glass of Baja wine, an acquired taste, or cold beer. And always cola for dessert. Not as the culinary crowning glory, but as a preventive measure against getting an upset tummie, also known as the "travelers curse" in these parts (during the course of our travels we replace the ineffectual cola with tequila – works much better!).

In the central section of Baja we cross a dusty semi-arid stretch dominated by yucca, agave and cactus plants. Hundreds of different types grow here, the most striking being the cardón, gigantic pillars which can grow up to 20 meters (66 feet) high. In the little oasis of San Ignacio we camp under date palms directly by the lavish clear waters known by the natives as "ojo de agua," Eye of Water. A former Jesuit mission, the little town has a picturesque tranquility.

Left: Every morning fishers at Playa Requesón bring in amazing quantities of rays.
Bottom left: A daily visitor – souvenir trader at Bahía Conception.

The old mission church on the plaza is well-preserved, the houses around it are colorful and neat, and we buy fresh dates from an old village woman. The wealthy yet sterile world of the United States lies far behind us, and we find ourselves in a world in reverse – poor, but crammed with delights for the senses!

Christmas is around the corner, and we plan to celebrate it at picturesque Playa Requesón on Bahía Concepcion to the east of the peninsula. We set up camp for the next few days at a shallow turquoise bay. Apart from us, the campground houses a few Canadians fleeing the winter cold of their home country. The sun glows out of a deep blue sky, warming the air to a perfect twenty-five degrees. Under a shady "palapa," a palm-frond shelter open on two sides, we gaze languidly at the crystalline water, read for hours at a stretch or write our diaries. We explore the surrounding waters in our canoe above water, and with snorkels below it. Pelicans hurl themselves into the waves in front of us on their hunt for fish, quarrelsome seagulls scream insults at each other and an occasional vulture glides silently past over our heads.

Not far from our camp, local fishermen sail out to sea every morning and return two hours later laden with their catch, chiefly ray. We buy two fillets but find the fibrous flesh hard to eat. I try my luck and, contrary to my expectations, am rewarded with a magnificent snapper, which we cook with plenty of garlic and olive oil. On Christmas Eve we decorate our palapa with shells, sarongs and candles, prepare a feast that matches our humble circumstances, and celebrate – the spirit is not particularly Christmassy,

Beach flotsam ...

*Above: San Miguel de Allende's eminent politicians greet the common people during a military parade. Right: Entrance portal of the cathedral at Zacatecas.*

but who needs it in a place like this? We sit around the campfire with the Canadians until late into the night, and not a single one of us feels the need to start humming "I'm dreaming of a white Christmas."

In La Paz, the capital of Baja, we board a rusty ferryboat that inspires little confidence but nevertheless deposits us safely at Mazatlán on the Mexican mainland after a sixteen-hour journey. Here we embark on our long climb to Mexico's central uplands. From sea level, a narrow serpentine road ascends to an altitude of over 2,800 meters (9,184 feet). Lucy good-humoredly carries us up into the mountains, as if the road were an old friend. The countryside is surprisingly green. Pines cluster so closely that they could almost be described as a forest. A vertical abyss yawns at intervals to our right, while to the left the cliff rises like a sheer wall. The scenery is magnificent, but we are so preoccupied with driving that we only notice it in passing. Heavy trucks, some in a scarily ramshackle condition, toil at walking pace up the hills or

roar kamikaze-style down the other side. In one of the countless blind curves, an enormous trailer rig comes towards us – on our side of the road. As the Mexicans say in these terrifying situations: "Ayyo!" We both spin our steering-wheels, Lucy bumps off the asphalt, the truck misses us by inches to our left while to our right the abyss threatens to engulf us, clouds of dust and stones fly up, our GPS is ripped from its holder, Sabine's cola and my adrenaline spill over, I counter steer in a panic, we feel asphalt under the wheels again, brake… Lucy stops and we take a deep breath! Made it!

Others weren't so lucky. Where other roads have crash barriers, here we see crosses rammed into the ground in memory of accident victims. The Mexicans call this road "El Espinazo del Diablo," or the Devil's backbone! We spend the night in El Salto at alpine altitude, finding a secure parking spot in a hotel courtyard on the edge of town. Tonight, we notice, all our airtight containers make a definite "pfffft" sound when we open them. Shower gel: "pfffft!", body lotion:

"pfffft!", olive oil: "pfffft!", yesterday's half-finished bottle of wine: "pfffft!". The air is thin up here, and excess pressure has built up inside the bottles as a result of the rapid ascent. As we say goodnight to each other with a quiet "pfffft," for once we don't attribute it to the obligatory refried beans we had for lunch … .

The road drops a little and levels out at around 2,000 meters (6,560 feet). We've reached Mexico's central upland, a bare, pale yellow landscape with a spring-like climate all year round. Winters are mild, summers are warm with some afternoon rain, and daytime temperatures rarely fall below twenty degrees or rise above thirty degrees: paradise for anyone sensitive to weather conditions. We cross the city boundary of Zacatecas in the late afternoon. Founded as early as 1546 by the Spaniards, this silver-mining town has retained its colonial atmosphere through the centuries. Twisting laneways are paved with rough cobble stones, "plazuelas" are fringed with monasteries, churches and magnificent townhouses. We

*The gulf between rich and poor is nowhere greater than in vain San Miguel de Allende.*

*Above: One tequila can't hurt – going to a bar in San Miguel de Allende.*
*Top right: Poultry stall at Zacatecas market.*

stroll through the center, designated a World Heritage Site, stand fascinated in front of the cathedral facade, an explosion of ornamentation, and explore new aromas and flavors at the countless market stalls and food sellers. An Indio is selling a drink out of earthenware jugs with which his donkey is laden. "Que es ese," we ask, "what is it?" "Agua miel," he answers – honey water – and because it sounds so innocuous we buy two mugs full, only to find that it doesn't taste of honey in the slightest. How could it? Days later we discover that it's made from a type of agave. Anyway, ten minutes later we're sitting in a bar ordering two tequilas and two cans of Coke to soothe our stomachs and our palates.

We buy a bag of "nopales" – freshly shredded cactus leaves with a subtly acidic flavor –

from an old market-woman and pick up some prawns at the fish store opposite; back in Lucy later that evening, we conjure up a delicious risotto out of these ingredients (plus a little garlic, onions, olive oil, broth, a touch of butter and our last Parmesan from the US) that erases the memory of the "aqua miel."

From our parking spot high above the old town in a hotel parking lot, we listen to the sounds of Mexico by night: dogs barking, engines roaring, a truck PA system in the distance; our parking lot's soundtrack featuring a tape loop of terrible orchestral arrangements of old Beatles songs, a nearby cockerel crowing at dead of night, a burglar alarm system going off every half-hour. Mexico is loud. Our journey through the country is like an endless assault on the

The colors of Mexico

senses: hearing, seeing, tasting, feeling, and smelling – everything is a little over the top. Lying in our bunks late at night, quite tired and very happy after the long day, we still have one unanswered question: is it the agave drink or the cactus leaves that's responsible for that almost inaudible "pffft"? …

San Miguel de Allende is an enchanting jewel among Mexico's colonial cities, and it's also the perfect spot to break our journey and learn some Spanish. It's time to spend some time sleeping in a proper bed, so we rent a little house in the historic center with a spacious bedroom, rambling kitchen and picturesque courtyard. Now we spend three hours every morning poring over our books, and our afternoons are devoted to homework. It's tough – the parts of our

brains responsible for learning languages have lain fallow for years and first need to be laboriously reactivated – but after seven weeks of grade-grubbing, we feel well enough prepared to conduct a halfway decent conversation in Spanish. Let's see how we get on.

After a brief detour through the mountains to the west of the capital, where we walk through clouds made up of millions of monarch butterflies in forests at an altitude of 3,000 meters (11,400 feet), we approach the seething cauldron of Mexico City. The oldest capital city in the New World is hemmed in by mighty chains of mountains 2,200 meters (7,216 feet) high. Once the area was occupied by Texcoco Lake, with an island in its midst which the Aztecs selected as the site of their capital Tenochtitlán. In its heyday the island was home to around 100,000 people, who erected a place described by its destroyer Hernán Cortés thus: "This city is so great and so beautiful that I can scarcely say half about it of all that I could, and even this little is almost incredible, for it is more beautiful than Granada …" Unfortunately, his perception

# Friday in San Miguel de Allende

"There's something magic about this place …!" breathes Alexandro in broken English, and he's deadly serious. A half-full glass of tequila stands in front of him on the greasy bar in "El Tenampa" – not his first this evening, to judge from his breath. Alexandro has slung a guitar across his stomach. When he is not sipping his tequila or talking about his city, he strums the strings. Then Gustavo joins in on his accordion, and Arthuro behind the bar raises his voice in bittersweet melancholy songs of love and friendship and their beautiful Mexico, their pride and joy. It is 11 pm. San Miguel is slowly closing down for the night. It was a long day; we left our cosy little house in Calle Organos in the center at nine-thirty in the morning:

Our route to the language school first leads down the bustling Calle Insurgentes, where ancient Mercedes buses rumble over the rough cobbles. Otherwise there's little going on. Mexicans like to start their day in a more leisurely manner.

The first market stallholders are only just setting up, and hardly any of the little stores behind the colorful facades open before ten. We turn into Calle Hidalgo, where the small Hotel Allende serves decent coffee *para llevar*, to go. The narrow lane rises to join the Jardín Principal, the city's main square set with shady jacaranda trees.

We cross the square and toil up Calle Correo to our goal at Number 46, Centro Bilingue. For the past three weeks we have had three hours of Spanish tuition here every day. Lupita, our teacher is not only a charming Mexican *señorita*; she also has the patience of the gods. When we manage to make the same grammar mistake for the tenth time in ten minutes, Lupita explains the rule once again with an almost unendurable patience. Her teaching style definitely brings results; our daily shopping is pretty successful after only a few days, and soon we can even make limited conversation.

Two rooms, kitchen and patio …: our new home in San Miguel

We leave school at one o'clock, starving. A few days ago we discovered a delightful small restaurant in the courtyard of a stately colonial building in Calle Mesones, which may very well become our local in the next three weeks. In the shade of ancient trees we sit on uncomfortable cast-iron chairs to eat grilled fish, stuffed tortillas or just a salad and drink a glass of Baja Chardonnay. In the launderette a few doors down we pick up the laundry we dropped off yesterday afternoon. Seven kilos of dirty washing are now clean and pressed, sealed neatly in plastic, for which we pay seventy pesos – not even six euros.

Continuing down Calle Mesones, we pass rows of elegant galleries and delicatessens. Not exactly typical of a Mexican upland town, but then San Miguel is not exactly typical: thanks to its internationally renowned art academy it has become the second home of many artists and art-lovers, and its ideal climate makes it a favorite with cultured American pensioners. This flow of hard US currency into the city has enabled the magnificent colonial architecture to be painstakingly restored and opulently decorated. At the same time, it has hewn a chasm between the prosperous foreigners and the poorer natives which is particularly evident in Calle Mesones. Mexicans don't go shopping here, the prices of designer clothes and sushi are at American levels, but the young store assistants still earn a salary of no more than the usual 160 US dollars per month and a cappuccino at the café around the corner would cost five per cent of their monthly salary. At the very bottom of the social scale, the old Indio women lead a pitiable life. Abandoned by their families, who have not infrequently headed to the US to seek their fortune, they sit at the curb and beg for a few pesos. They are wretched souls in a city in which, so it appears, two parallel worlds attempt to coexist without coming too close to each other.

*Blood-stained ritual: bullfighting in San Miguel de Allende.*

Tinny music echoes from Calle San Francisco, down which a procession honoring one of the countless saints is slowly moving towards the Jardín, the faithful led by a brass band. Their understanding of music is primarily limited to volume; the louder they play, the closer they are to heaven. They are followed by a group chiefly composed of older men and women, holding candles and piously threading their way through the lanes. Not a week goes by in San Miguel without a procession. And if it's not the church that's celebrating it's the military, marching briskly through the streets to commemorate some Mexican freedom fighter or other. Fiesta Mexicana!

It's time to go home. How lucky we've been with our little house in Calle Organos. We hadn't booked any accommodation in advance before we came to San Miguel. The town is said to be booked out in January, and when we arrived it seemed that we would have to live at the campground. But by chance we discovered a little real estate management office, where jolly, plump Enrique sat behind a desk piled impressively high with files. We told him of our plight, and he actually offered us this one-storey house at a reasonable price. It is designed in typically Mexican style; the heart of the house is an open patio, a courtyard with a little fountain around which the

69

living-room, two bedrooms, kitchen and a roofed veranda are grouped. To get from the bedroom to the kitchen we have to cross the open courtyard. It's wonderful! We're living like kings in our very own little palace.

In the early evening I pack the camera, lenses and tripod and set off through the town to the old bullring. Sabine refuses to attend the spectacle – and she proves to be right.

In the center of town stands an old arena with seating for 3000. The event is sold out and I am surprised to see that the crowd is almost entirely made up of Mexicans. A little brass band creates a party atmosphere, while tacos with chili sauce or lemon juice are sold and washed down with beer or red wine or tequila. Proud *hombres* in pointed-toe cowboy boots, elegant *sombreros* on their heads, stride in the company of fiery *chicas* wearing such huge earrings that turning their heads becomes a real challenge. The air smells of salsa, perfume, horses and *cerveza* – a pretty explosive mixture.

*I'm still working on the mustache ...*

The rules at the *Corrida del Toros* are draconian, ritualistic and cruel. At the start of the event, the participants enter the arena and bow to the audience. Tonight belongs to the *picadores*, the lance-bearers. The fight comprises three sections, each announced by trumpet fanfares.

First the picador wounds the bull in the neck with his lance, a move intended to enrage the bull not weaken it. In the second part, the torero stabs the poor creature in the back with banderillas, barbed wands decorated with ribbons which stick in the wound. In the third and final part of the fight the bull is once again provoked into attacking before the picador finally drives his dagger deep into the blood-covered animal's neck, between the shoulder-blades, attempting to reach the heart. He fails in all four fights, and each time an assistant – I'll call him "butcher" – is forced to put a merciful end to the spectacle with a well-placed thrust of his dagger to the bull's neck.

And the cruelty doesn't end there. The picador is awarded one or both ears of the bull as a trophy and does a lap of honor around the arena, the audience accompanying his progress with frantic cheering as the señoras throw their perfumed handkerchiefs down to him and the señores their sombreros. While this goes on the dead bull is dragged out of the arena by a powerful horse and the band plays a lively paso doble.

This ritual slaughter going under the name of "fight" takes around twenty minutes. The picador conveys himself as proud and courageous, assuming respect for the bull, while in reality celebrating the cowardly, humiliating execution of a helpless creature which never had a chance in the first place.

I have to admit that the atmosphere in this old arena – the music, the shouts and cheers, the smells, the beautiful women, the bloody scenes of battle – touch an atavistic nerve in me which makes me shout "olé" in euphoria as well. And yet, notwithstanding instinct, culture and tradition, the bullfight is the bloody consummation of a fit of childish, macho behavior and should be banned!

On my way home through the dark lanes of San Miguel de Allende the town appears as the perfect setting for a melancholy road movie. The feeble street lights cast bizarre shadows on the ancient walls, and the wind plays with a discarded newspaper, tossing it ahead of me like a dancer. I cross the Jardín de Principal, stroll down Calle Recreo to Calle Mesones and hear music from a little bar with real saloon doors.

A tequila can't do any harm after all the bloodlust, I think, and go inside. And there they are: Alexandro with his guitar, Gustavo with his accordion, Arthuro behind the bar, all gazing at me as if they'd been waiting for me all along!

Calle Correo in San Miguel de Allende

of the city's beauty did not prevent him from first conquering it, then razing it to the ground in 1521 and building a new city in its place; not half a millennium later, the new city would become the largest megalopolis on the planet. No-one knows the exact population of Greater Mexico City for sure. The majority of estimates quote twenty to over thirty million people. Of course, the Aztecs' island would be far too small to fit all these inhabitants, so that over the years Lake Texcoco was drained to provide more space. However, this idea went badly wrong: today, Mexico City has no water supply of its own. Although the city's daily consumption of the precious liquid is twice as high as in Germany at over 300 liters per capita, Lake Texcoco is now dry and Río Lerma, the city's water source in the

*Field studies!*

past, is nothing but a trickle. Every day, a volume of water far exceeding one billion liters has to be pumped up a steep rise of 1,000 meters (3,280 feet) from Presa Valle de Bravo, a reservoir 150 kilometers (90 miles) away, before it can flow across the mountains enclosing the Valley of Mexico – an enormously energy-intensive process. "The city once built in the water by the Aztecs," our guidebook informs us, "will eventually become uninhabitable owing to its lack of water."

We plan to approach Mexico City cautiously – but here too, something goes very wrong. A toll ring road runs at a respectable distance from the city, and we take it with the intention of going to Teotihuacán, a site of ancient ruins to the north of Mexico City. Somewhere, somehow, we miss a turn-off, a sign, an exit – whatever – and fail to notice our mistake until it's too late. We are in the jaws of the fiend, and have hopelessly lost any sense of orientation. It's three in the afternoon, the evening rush-hour is just starting and we are crushed in its grip like the

Left page, top:
Monarch butterflies
near the mountain
village of San Luis,
Mexico.
Left: At the Sun Pyra-
mid in Teotihuacan.
Bottom: Sun Stone
from the Aztecs'
main temple in
their capital of
Tenochtitlán, today
Mexico City.

coils of a python. Our nervousness grows. We have no maps that could help us; only our satellite navigation system gives a vague idea of where we are. A north-bound road marked in red appears on the display – we'll take it. But try though we might, we can't find the exit, and wander aimlessly through small side streets. Our GPS tell us that we should be on the middle of a highway – but darn it, there's no highway here!! Instead, we're faced with hooting VW Beetles, locals full of curiosity and an impenetrable labyrinth of streets ... God help us ...!!!

Six hours later we arrive at San Juan de Teotihuacán campsite. Darkness has already fallen, and our nerves are in shreds after driving a mere 80 nightmarish kilometers (48 miles) in those six hours. Although we're at an impressive altitude of 2,200 meters (7,216 feet), this is the low point of our journey for time being.

We spend the next morning lazing around, enjoying a well-earned rest at the campground before finally taking a taxi to the ruins in the afternoon. Teotihuacán is considered the most significant cultural center of Old America. Believed to have been founded in 100 B.C., in its heyday between 200 and 500 A.D. its 22 square kilometers (8 square miles) were home to an estimated 200,000 people. The majority of the area is still untouched and lies unexcavated; but even the sheer scale of what is accessible is breathtaking.

Two pyramids tower over Teotihuacán. At the northern end of the area's main axis, known as *Calzada de los Muertos*, the mighty Moon Pyramid rises 45 meters (148 feet) into the sky. We clamber up its ancient stone ashlars to the top, and are rewarded by a magnificent view over the ruins and the mountains surrounding them. The star of Teotihuacán, however, is the

Fortress-like Zócalo Cathedral on the main square in Mexico City, believed to be the biggest in America.

Sun Pyramid, in the central area of the north-south axis. With sides of 200 meters (656 feet) in length and 70 meters (230 feet) high, it is the third largest pyramid in the world. Both pyramids were primarily religious centers and mausoleums; but what kind of a people would create such a vast cult site? Research yields little information. Where these people came from, the language they spoke, the structure of their society and their ultimate fate – all shrouded in mystery. We do not even know the name the inhabitants gave to their city. When centuries later the Aztecs founded their empire and rose to become the rulers of Mesoamerica, the city was already an abandoned ruin. Yet the newcomers were convinced that only extraterrestrial beings could have erected a site of such magnificence, and gave the ruins the name they still bear today: Teotihuacán, "home of the gods."

The next morning we pack a few clothes, toothbrush and earplugs into a rucksack, grab our camera and credit card and board a bus which takes us to Mexico City, leaving Lucy behind at the secure campground. In the center of the city, near the main square or Zócalo, we find a plain but cheap room, move in for three nights and set out to make our peace with Mexico City. What's the best way to approach a city which contains a simply overwhelming range of sights spanning the epochs and the centuries? With an espresso on the roof patio of "Hotel Majestic" at the north-western corner of Zócalo, of course! We gaze down at the largest and oldest city square on the American continent. Its asphalt-gray surface may not be as picturesque as that of the Jardín in San Miguel de Allende (no green in sight apart from the omnipresent Beetle taxis), but it's steeped in history and is a symbol of Mexican identity. Under an enormous green,

Anthropological Museum and Frida Kahlo's birthplace) and folk events (ballet in the Palacio de Bellas Artes and street dancers on Zócalo), and stroll through markets (in the delightful Coyoacan district), all interspersed with culinary journeys of discovery in elegant restaurants or funky street vendors. In the days of our stay, we experience a city as fragmented as its history is fascinating: repulsive and charming, poverty-stricken and glamorous, terrifying and endearing – probably as full of contradictions as the Mexican soul itself. A memorial plaque commemorating the decline of the Aztec Tenochtitlán in what is today the district of Tlatelolco reflects this polarity, proclaiming "On 13 August 1521 Tlatelolco, heroically defended by Cuauhtemoc, fell into the hands of Hernán Cortés. It was neither a victory nor a defeat, but the painful birth of the mestizo people, of today's Mexico."

white and red flag, indigenas dance *concheros* that depict the Aztec past. Grubby children in torn clothes beg for a couple of pesos, while a little further on, snobs dressed up to the nines alight from a white stretch limo.

Our days in Mexico City give us little time to draw breath; we tour magnificent colonial houses and Aztec ruins (the cathedral and the main temple), visit museums (the outstanding

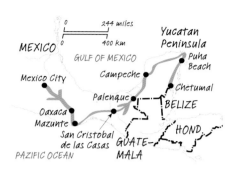

# Mexico's South: Mayan Heartland

"If only one place on earth could be awarded the title of paradise, that place would be Mexico."
*Alexander von Humboldt*

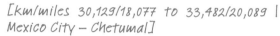

[km/miles 30,129/18,077 to 33,482/20,089 | Mexico City – Chetumal]

*Young dancer in colonial Oaxaca.*

Instead of a Wild West, Mexico has a Wild South. Its Indian heartbeat is unmistakable in the provinces of Oaxaca and Chiapas. We drive around Mexico City once again, this time going east (and successfully) on the MEX 190, a well-constructed toll road which again climbs to over 3,000 meters (9840 feet) in parts. A view of the two awe-inspiring volcanoes Iztaccíhuatl (5,230 m / 17,154 ft) and Popocatépetl (5,452 m /17,883 ft) should accompany us along this stretch; however, both are invisible behind the capital's thick veil of smog, and what isn't obscured by the smog has no chance against the dust-laden west wind.

We traverse barren landscapes of cactus and agave before reaching the old colonial city of Oaxaca after two days of moderately paced driving. From there we turn onto the twisting MEX 175, which takes us across a final mountain range after 250 kilometers (150 miles) and seven (!) hours before descending to the Pacific coast. The route is tortuous, but the landscape around us is jaw-dropping: surrounded by arid semi-desert on the north side of the mountains, we emerge in the south into a lush, green tropical world. A smell of mold hangs in the moist, heavy air, and the road unfurls past plantations of sugarcane, bananas and coffee.

By nightfall we have already reached our destination, the little fishing village of Mazunte at the beach of the same name. We find a parking spot behind Yuri's beach restaurant between roaming hens, a line of flapping bedsheets and a tortilla oven. Despite the high temperatures, the night is bearable. Thanks to Lucy's excellent insulation, the cab is still bathed in the cool air of the upland plain, and we fall asleep rapidly. Early the next morning, just as the sun is struggling above the horizon, I creep out of the cab, laden with the camera bag, and am taking a few photos of the still-deserted beach, of palm trees and empty lounge chairs in the flat morning light when a couple of fishermen appear. They stand on the shore, appraise the incoming waves and fling out their nets as if to an inaudible command, only to draw them in again immediately. It's a simple technique with an impressive success rate; in less than fifteen minutes each of them has caught enough to feed the whole family, probably with enough left over for all their friends, relations and pets. I start a conversation with Silvano. It's hard to guess his age – perhaps around forty. Unlike the others, he seems to enjoy being photographed. We chat about fishing, smoking weed, sea-turtles and the lightness of being, drink a sleepy coffee with Yuri as he opens up his beach store, and later go to the home of Silvano's 76-year-old mother. Here he has built himself a little hut in the yard, where he has lived for several years. In front of his hut stands a rough wooden frame threaded with yarn on which he weaves hammocks. He does a roaring trade with the backpackers on the beach, selling his work for at least 100 pesos, or

eight euros; the first price he quotes is 300. If he works steadily without stopping, he can finish a hammock in a day – but he rarely does, preferring to spend the afternoons sitting in the shade of the palm trees with his friends, sipping a "Sol" and rolling a joint. Anyone that can effortlessly bring home bucketfuls of fish from the sea on their doorstep, has no worries about heating bills and does not need a television leads a far more carefree life! For the rest of the day, the heat prevents any unnecessary movement. We lie on the beach, read, paddle in the Pacific, chat, sleep – in fact, we "do a Silvano" (the only thing we leave out is the joint).

The next day we leave Mazunte, heading east along the coast and soon ascending once more into the cooler hinterland, to the little town of San Cristóbal de las Casas in the province of Chiapas. Here we are finally at the heart of the Mayan world, which will accompany us over the next weeks as far as Honduras. The surrounding villages are populated by Tzotziles und Tzeltales, the largest Mayan ethnic groups in Chiapas. They meet in the town in the early morning to sell their agricultural produce or crafts at the "mercado municipal,"

*Above: Silvano drinks his morning coffee at Yuri's beach restaurant in Mazunte.*
*Left: Sunrise at Mazunte beach.*

Tropical Mexico: Agua Azul Falls in the steamy, humid lowlands of Chiapas.

trailed by a horde of begging children and hunched indigenous women. San Cristóbal de las Casas is perhaps the most attractive of all Mexico's cities, despite its lack of outstanding architectural highlights; a fascinating mixture of Indian heritage and colonial history gives the town its special character, while also revealing the social problems of Mexico's south. Poverty is widespread and illiteracy, unemployment and infant mortality are high. Aid funds seep into the pockets of corrupt officials and party bigwigs. Large tracts of cultivatable land are owned by only a few mestizos, who also hold the political reins. The "indigena" are frequently reduced to leading grim lives as landless peasants, coffee pickers or itinerant laborers.

At Zócalo, the main square, we meet Caesar, a mestizo who organizes tours into villages in the outlying mountains for tourists. We and four other travelers board his old VW bus and drive to Chamula, twelve kilometers (7 miles)

away, a religious center for the Tzotzil living there and in the surrounding area. From the village entrance we walk past the graveyard to the village center, taking in the dwelling of a "mayordomos," a religious and social leader whose main room houses an altar crammed with relics; our next stop is to a family of weavers hoping to sell us some of their attractive fabrics. Caesar gravely recounts tales of religious and social customs, healing rituals and shamanism, social conflicts and the political struggle of the indigenas for more self-determination and fair land reforms. He brings us to the market square, and finally to the 19th-century Catholic church. We enter a mystical place; this is not a church in the conventional sense of the word. There are no pews, organ, pulpit and confessionals: instead, the bare tiled floor is covered with hundreds of candles, whose light bathes the interior in a mysterious twilight. Kneeling indigenas mumble prayers before wooden statues of Catholic saints

which have taken over the functions of the Mayans' old nature gods. An old woman waves a live chicken first over the candles, then above the heads of her fellow worshipers, before wringing its neck. Empty Coke bottles cover the floor. The beverage is drunk as a part of religious procedures because belching drives away evil spirits. The air is heavy with the scent of incense. Here, ancient Mayan rituals are mingled with the rites of the Catholic Church. We feel we have been transported to another world which moves and disturbs us in equal measure. The church at Chamula will have a more profound and sustained effect on us than almost anywhere else we encounter on our travels.

The MEX 199 curves down into the steamy heat of the tropics. The Mexican army has set up checkpoints in an attempt to combat Indian rebels. Our guide warns us of brigands and bandits, but instead we see laughing Maya children and women waving in front of wooden hovels. We arrive in Yucatán, between the Gulf of Mexico and the Caribbean, home to the country's most awe-inspiring Mayan sites and also its most beautiful beaches. But these benefits have their consequences; the peninsula has been overrun by American package tourists. In the grid-plan city of Cancun on the Caribbean coast, the 22 kilometers (13 miles) of "zona hotelera" alone contain 143 hotels with a total of 26,200 rooms. The city registered over three million visitors in

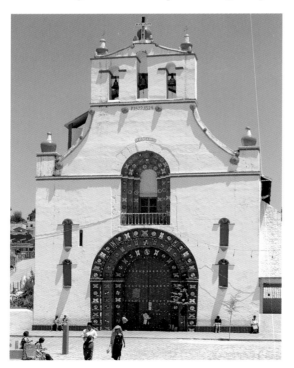

Fabric store in San Lorenzo
Zinacantán

*Above: Temple of the Inscriptions at Palenque, Yucatán.*
*Right: Under waving palms – campground in Chetumal Bay, Yucatán.*
*Top right: Pyramid of Uxmal in Yucatán.*

2000, generating one-third of the country's total tourist revenues.

And so we take our place in endless lines of tourists, visit the ruins in the jungle at Palenque, the mighty temples of Chichén Itzá, the masterfully constructed pyramids at Uxmal and the ceremonial site of Tulum at its glorious coastal location – stone witnesses to a vanished kingdom of the Maya, which at the zenith of its power must have numbered ten million people. The Maya erected magnificent religious buildings, developed a unique form of script, a sophisticated calendar system and complex mathematical systems; they possessed an astonishing wealth of astronomical knowledge, and used the course of Venus to observe the fluctuations in the earth's rotational axis at a time when the teachings of the European Church still proclaimed that the earth was flat. And yet in the 9th century this advanced and mighty culture gradually began to

crumble, for reasons which are still shrouded in mystery. By the time the Spaniards arrived in the 16th century, almost all the great Maya settlements were deserted. What could the causes have been? Over-population? Ecological collapse? Climate disaster? Political weakness? Decadence and degeneracy? Nobody knows. But

in the shadow of all the vast palaces and temples we visit in Yucatán, the intermittent sadness in the present fate of Mexico's indigenous populations takes on an even more tragic dimension.

We spend our last days in Mexico on the beach of Xpu-Ha, to the south of Cancún. 50 meters (164 feet) below our parking spot, the Caribbean waves roll into the broad sweep of the bay. By day, the water glows in such a clear turquoise that we could almost believe that Itzamaná, the Mayan god of creation, had spilt a bucket of precious oil paint into the bay in an access of high spirits. The Yucatán sky is a pure, clear blue. Although menacing clouds build up along the horizon every afternoon, they keep their distance without blocking the sun's view. A sensation of farewell hangs in the tropical air. In a few days we will leave Mexico after spending almost four months here. We found a country that is dazzling, but also has its areas of

shadow; the people we met were poor and full of vitality, rough and enchanting; we were welcomed as guests, yet still remained outsiders from another world. The cultural and material gulf between guest and host is so broad that unlike the United States or Canada, contacts were hard to establish and are unlikely to survive beyond our meetings. We leave Mexico without collecting a single address apart from that of our Spanish teacher; and yet we have collected "baggage" crammed with powerful, unforgettable experiences. Mexico has a strange, contradictory magic which we are unable to fathom fully and which occupies us in those days on the beach at Xpu-Ha. A phenomenon we feel compelled to explore in more depth – and we're certain that one day we will. But for now it's hasta la vista, México!

Last days in Xpu-Ha

Mayan ruins at Tulum on Yucatán's Caribbean coast

# Northern Central America: Sunken Worlds

*"To the car mechanic: 'Give me a new horn – much louder than the one I have.' – 'What for?' – 'Because my brakes don't work!'"*

*Latin American joke*

[km/miles 33,482/20,089 to 36,501/21,900|
Chetumal – Choluteca]

*Above: Watch out – city buses in Guatemala. Opposite page: Enchanting Guatemala – proud women in the streets of Antigua.*

All of Central America was colonized by the Spaniards. But wait! All of it? No! A tiny strip of tropical country between today's Mexico and Guatemala became part of the British Empire, initially in cultural and traditional terms, but eventually fully official. In 1981 it achieved independence and since then has borne the name Belize.

Our border crossing is uneventful – a sluggish process, but practiced and straightforward. Anyway, it's much too hot for a full vehicle search. Although one thing did strike us at the border: on the Belize side the people are relaxed, friendly and ultra-cool – no dark mutterings, no Mexican hyperactivity – and they all speak English, the official language in Belize. A few kilometers across the border, at the end of Chetumal Bay, is the little town of Corozal. We drive through sleepy streets to the beach, to the sound of reggae music pumping out of many of the simple single-story wooden houses. Behind the open doors, people are lounging in hammocks taking a siesta.

No doubt about it – we're definitely in the Caribbean. At the shore, dark-skinned children play in the filthy water. A beach bar is open for business; we sit at the counter and order a "Bilkini," the only brand of beer readily available in Belize's bars – so we'd better get used to it straight away.

After our break, we speed along the hundred or so kilometers (60 miles) to Belize City. We pass three police road blocks on the narrow highway into the capital. At two of them we produce our papers and are waved on; at the third, Lucy is searched for weapons and drugs. It's annoying and delays us. When we finally reach Belize City, it's too late to find a suitable parking spot for the night, so we take a room in "Great Place" Hotel (such an imaginative name …). At sunset we stroll through the city center, which is pretty unattractive. Rattletrap Japanese pickups maneuver through narrow lanes, dreadlocked street sellers at ramshackle stalls peddle jewelry and wood-carvings, mestizos whip up filled tortillas and reggae throbs at a painful volume from a CD store. We're offered marihuana at every corner, and eventually we have the strange feeling that absolutely everyone must be stoned. The jewelry vendor: stoned! The street laborer: stoned! The traffic cop: stoned! The children playing at the bridge: all stoned! Our impression is accompanied by the sixty-four thousand dollar question, "What are we actually doing here?" But the garden of the hotel restaurant provides the answer: eating a delicious lunch!

At "Caesar's Place," a little campground over to the west of the country, we establish a kind of base camp for the next few days. We find a shady spot under a tree, set up a rain shelter

Head held high: toucan in the forest in Belize

just in case and seek relief from the heat by repeatedly heading down to the river to swim.

The Easter holidays are around the corner, and we need to stock up on supplies. In nearby San Ignacio we buy fresh fruit and vegetables at the market and delicious wholegrain bread at Joseph and Helen's "German Bakery." The couple left their German region of Franconia one year ago for financial reasons and emigrated to West Belize. We try to get our heads round the idea of German bakers leaving their homeland because they can't envisage having financial security for the future – and finding it in Belize, a country where an estimated thirty percent of the population lives below the poverty line. Joseph and Helen's store is a little German enclave. The display counter and café furnishings apparently come from their bakery in Upper Franconia, trays of hazelnut danishes and cherry cake

and more stand around fresh from the oven, and the scent …!

The next morning we make an early start, planning to take a rough, twisting track into the wild jungle of Mountain Pine Ridge Forest Reserves and explore the Mayan ruins of Caracol at their heart. Around 1,400 years ago, we read, some 150,000 people lived in an area of 88 square kilometers (33 square miles), a population hardly smaller than the whole of Belize today. But rapacious nature snatched back the land, and today only a few of the ancient buildings have been uncovered. The track leading there is stony and dusty, and the high temperatures are a burden both for us and for Lucy. At first we pass through Mayan villages where children race after us, their fathers risking an inquisitive glance from under their deeply tipped straw hats. Then we plunge into a tropical wilderness. The lush forest positively steams with humidity, a toucan flies directly past our windscreen and the insects make such a loud clatter that I some-

times wonder whether Lucy's wheel bearings are giving up. Soon we will reach some waterfalls where we plan to take a break. But suddenly we hear a clattering noise which definitely doesn't come from a cricket. We drive off the track and investigate: a shock absorber mount has snapped and the shock absorber is flapping around in the wheel arch. We can't go on. I dismantle the shock absorber in the sweltering heat, we turn around and drive the 50 kilometers (30 miles) back to San Ignacio at a snail's pace.

At the edge of town is a garage where the broken mount could be welded in no time. But it's Easter Saturday, and no-one will get their hands dirty again before Tuesday – what bad luck! Annoyed, we return to Caesar's Place and set up camp again after only packing up the same morning. We go for a swim in the river, dress in clean clothes and later sit at the restaurant's open-air bar. Darkness falls swiftly in tropical Belize. Crickets chirp, a giant cucaracha lurches across the counter and in the distance we hear the ominous roar of monkeys. Sabine looks delightful in her linen top and the new earrings she bought in Mexico. We drink a Caribbean cocktail of coconut rum and pineapple juice, bearing the intriguing name of "panty-ripper"… perhaps this messed-up day might have a happy ending after all!

We cross Caracol off our plans. On the Tuesday after Easter we have the mount welded and take the opportunity to order four new shock absorbers. By Wednesday we're ready to start for Guatemala and cross the border at Benque Viejo del Carmen, again mastering the formalities without difficulty. Whoever told us that border crossings in Central America would be annoying and time-consuming? We drive west, initially following rough dirt roads that lead through tropical hills scarred by barren areas of pasture. El Petén, as Guatemala's thinly populated most northerly administrative region is called, is the seventh largest rainforest reserve in the world. But a settlement program organ-

*Left page: In Belize – just outside Corozal we stock up on fresh fruit from a roadside vendor.*
*Top left and right: Cool but hot – young Afro-Caribbeans in Belize.*

ized by the government is bringing the fragile ecosystem to the point of collapse. Day by day new settlers arrive, clearing the forest using slash-and-burn methods. The track we are following is flanked only by scant remnants of the primeval rainforest.

After around 70 kilometers (42 miles), by now over ultra-smooth asphalt, we turn north; another hour's drive brings us to Tikal, once the Mayans' greatest ceremonial centers. We find a secure spot for the night directly at the entrance to the site and early next morning, an hour before sunrise, we are standing at the gateway to the ruins, where a guide awaits us – essential for us to be permitted to enter the site at this hour. Armed with headlamps, we file through the dark tropical forest past ancient walls, the steep slopes of pyramids, vast ceremonial squares and finely chiseled columns, greeted by strident lion-like roars from howler monkeys high in the trees above. After forty-five minutes we reach

Temple IV and examine it in the first diffuse fingers of daylight. At the top, we sit on historic stone ashlars to await the sunrise. The pyramids overshadow the dense roof of leaves above us; the jungle is swathed in damp morning mist. Exotic birdsong echoes from the depths of the forest, and the whoops of the monkeys resound like a hymn to creation. Then the first rays of the

Pig farmers make
their laborious way to
the livestock market
at Chichicastenango.

sun break through a gap in the cloudy sky, reaching down to touch Tikal. We are motionless and moved, experiencing truly otherworldly moments at the peak of Pyramid IV: a new day dawns in a mystical, sunken world!

En route to the uplands, poverty-stricken Guatemala surprises us with flawless asphalt roads and a first-class network of gas stations including clean toilets (with paper, working flush mechanisms and – something we hadn't seen for a long time – toilet seats!). But nevertheless the drive is torment. We labor upwards along tortuous, twisting curves, ascending from sea-level to an altitude of 2,200 meters (7,216 feet). Cross-country buses, some in thoroughly antiquated condition, race along the road as if there were no tomorrow. They are colorfully painted and often have a statue of the Virgin Mary in the windshield, watching over their murderous progress. Apparently trusting blindly in God, their crazy drivers overtake any vehicle in their

path, following a professional code which seems to be widespread throughout Latin America. How irresponsible must they be, in what contempt must they hold human life, to expose their passengers to such dangers? We will pass three bus accidents with fatalities before we reach Chile.

We take a three-day stopover in the old colonial town of Antigua. Formerly Guatemala's capital, it is overshadowed by three volcanoes: Fuego, Agua and Acatenango. We stroll down its roughly cobbled streets past colossal colonial buildings. At one time Antigua was a town of chapels, convents, monasteries and churches. Here "…one feels the urgent desire to sin," wrote Guatemalan author Miguel Angel Asturias. We know the feeling; instead of exploring churches, museums and volcanoes, we're drawn to backyard restaurants and farmers' markets, park benches and Internet cafés. We succumb to the lure of dalliance. And because this

picturesque town offers a bewildering choice of such worldly sites between its museum-like facades, we love it all the more.

To the west of Antigua, half a day's drive away through the mountains, we arrive at the basin of Lago de Atitlán, perhaps one of the world's most beautiful natural landscapes. Enclosed by perfectly formed volcanoes, its waters "glitter like molten silver" (in the words of explorer John Lloyd Stephens), and its southern and south-eastern banks are fringed by little villages clinging to steep mountain slopes, with bustling markets at the feet of old colonial churches. Perfect subjects for an obsessive photographer, you might think; but during our visit, apart from a few brief moments Lago Atitlán is shrouded in the hazy mist that presages the rainy season. My camera stays in its case, my photographer's soul in agony. We take a boat and spend a day touring, visiting Mayan villages where women in colorful traditional costume sell finely woven fabrics, children beg for a few quezales and men hold fire rituals before squat colonial churches. And in the hazy distance, we are per-

petually accompanied by the volcano that overshadows everything like a sentinel: Tolimán. A strange vibration fills the air. We have the odd feeling that we are in safe hands, as if, despite the dullness of the weather, we are in the right place at the right time. And our hunch proves to be right …!

# Protective Powers

Immediately after Panajachel we ascend an endless series of curves up to an altitude of almost 2,700 meters (8,856 feet). The road switchbacks through forests and deeply slashed valleys; we will soon be at our day's destination, the mountain village of Chichicastenango in the department of El Quiché, where we plan next day to visit the Mayan market that's famous far beyond the boundaries of the province. One steep descent lies ahead. Lucy has had a punishing day today, but she's nearly there. I need to brake before going into a bend, hit the pedal and … go right through to the floor. The brakes have failed! My heart stops. The road before us plunges down the mountainside, to the right is a sheer drop, to the left dense forest. I spin the wheel round instinctively, bounce off the road at a teetering angle, hit the side road and use the handbrake to bring Lucy to a standstill only centimeters in front of a heavy metal gate. Who the heck in this deserted spot would set up a metal gate that could stop a tank? We stare at the iron wall before us, frozen in shock. Sabine is as pale as a cloudy sky over Lago Atitlán.

At Chichicastenango market

What happened? The brakes didn't overheat, we would have smelt it. The brake fluid reservoir is full to the brim, and the brake pads were replaced in Santa Fé around 10,000 kilometers (6,000 miles) ago. A farmer with a grim expression and a machete at his belt marches up the road. We ask him how far the next village is and where we can find a garage. There's a gas station 2 kilometers (1,2 miles) down the road, he informs us, and I set off. The gas station has no mechanic, but there is a garage nearby. I knock at a dented metal door. After never-ending minutes a short Maya opens the door, gazing in bewilderment at my Western features. I describe the problem as best I can in my broken Spanish, and he tells me in kindly tones to wait at the truck until he comes. One hour later he rumbles up the mountain in an old pickup and examines the brakes. He doesn't take long to discover that the main brake cylinder is faulty. We will have to drive Lucy down to his garage. Very funny (I start to formulate in my limited Spanish), how can we do that with no brakes? But before the words can leave my lips he's climbed back into his clattering pickup and roared off. In four-wheel drive mode and reduced first gear ratio, with sweating hands and hammering heart, we crawl down the mountain at walking pace. The gear reduction is remarkably effective at braking Lucy's four-ton weight and the handbrake takes care of the rest, so that after an eternity we actually arrive in one piece at Anegletto's garage – that's the name of our savior. We park between rusty jalopies and piles of scrap. "No problema!" assures Anegletto; "mañana," during the course of tomorrow the brakes will be repaired. We're wary about believing him. We take a room at the "Maya Inn" hotel in the center of Chichicastenango and spend a restless night with images of steeply sloping roads, futile attempts at braking and yawning abysses pursuing us into our dreams. The next day around lunchtime, we visit Anegletto's garage again and … there stands Lucy, fully repaired and ready to go with a brand-new main brake cylinder. We're stunned. Early that morning (a Sunday!), Anegletto had driven his old pickup to Santa Cruz del Quiché 20 kilometers (12 miles) away and found the right part. He presents us with a bill for the equivalent of less than 200 euros – a large sum in the mountains of Guatemala; but it's all I can do not to kiss the oil-covered hands of this kindly man. I refrain, and reward him with a generous tip. In all this excitement, the actual reason for our visit to the remote mountain region has almost receded into the background, but that would be doing Chichicastenango an injustice. The bustling market, which extends throughout the entire village, is packed with colorful, fascinating activity which – despite the streams of tourists moving through the narrow lanes – forms an unforgettable pageant. In the evening Chichicastenango quietens down, and so do we. We sit in the hotel bar drinking Chilean red wine, in our thoughts toasting Anegletto – and the divine powers that protected us in the right place, at the right time.

# Southern Central America: Looking for the Sacred Bird

"There are five directions. You, right here, are the fifth point of the compass."

*Humberto Ak'abal, Mayan poet from Guatemala*

[km/miles 36,501/ 21,901 to 39,997/23,998| Choluteca – Puerto Viejo]

*Tropical luxuriance: heliconia on Costa Rica's Caribbean coast*

We enter Honduras at a small border crossing in the east of Guatemala's hill country. Here, the process is rather more confusing – for all those involved, as far as we can see. Nobody really knows what to do about this German truck, and the scooter on the back doesn't exactly help the proceedings. But after an hour we're in Honduras. Immediately to the east of the border, we visit the spectacular Mayan ruins at Copán. What makes our jaws drop is not an array of mighty pyramids or temple buildings, but a series of artistically carved portrait stelae and, most impressive of all, the Hieroglyphic Stairway – the longest stone-carved Mayan text in existence. Its sixty-three stone steps recount the history of Copán in over 2,200 characters. Sadly, parts of the stairway are so eroded that they are illegible. Leaving Copán, we bid farewell to the world of the Maya. The site is the southernmost outpost of a culture which has fascinated us with its mysteries throughout the last months of our journey, not only because of its significant historical status.

We travel north-east along Honduras' Caribbean coastline on solid roads with moderate traffic. Both of us are afflicted yet again by a stomach upset, so that traveling is not exactly fun. In the hinterland of the Caribbean, not far from the little town of La Ceiba set between the

tropical forests which fringe Rio Cangrejal, we arrive at "Omega Jungle Lodge" run by Udo, of German descent, and his partner Sylvia. The perfect place to recuperate! Fourteen years ago, this part of the world was the last outpost in Udo's search for the perfect rafting area. He bought a plot of land near the river and set up a one-man river rafting operation, which by now has grown into a respectable company with numerous employees. We spend a few days loafing around in a lovingly decorated "cabaña" and then subject our stomachs' newly regained health to a tough test – a Category IV river rafting tour through the rapids of the Río Cangrejal. What fun! Our Japanese tour guide Azushi is a really nice guy and does a great job – he just needs to work a little on his pronunciation of "river-rafting" ("livel-lafting").

From the Caribbean shore we burn rubber to the capital of Honduras, Tegucigalpa. The city has nothing to offer transit travelers, so that we continue along steep tracks to La Tigra National Park only 20 kilometers (12 miles) to the north. At an altitude of just under 2,300 meters (7,544 feet), the forests here are home to hosts of rare fauna, and provide a habitat for pumas, anteaters, ocelots, peccaries and opossums. But we're attracted by one particular bird: the quetzal, probably the most beautiful, and certainly

the rarest, of all Central American species of bird. The quetzal was regarded as sacred by the Maya and the Aztecs, and its tail feathers, which grow up to one meter (3,28 feet) long, were sometimes prized more highly than gold. Ever since the tropical forests of Yucatán we have been fruitlessly hoping to catch a glimpse of a quetzal. It is said to be found here in La Tigra

National Park in this season, according to our guidebook. The afternoon of our arrival already sees us tramping down narrow pathways in an elfen wood of liana, bushes and gigantic ferns. We hear rustling in the undergrowth and unfamiliar birdsong in the high tree crowns, are forced to use a branch to beat a path through the thick cobwebs stretched between moss-grown tree trunks – but we never spot a single quetzal. The next morning shortly after sunrise, we again make for the deserted forest in the cool of the morning, to return hours later unsuccessfully to our camp. No sign of a quetzal.

From the highlands of Honduras we descend to the Pacific coast, where we are received by humid heat and tropical storms. We reach the Nicaraguan border near the village of El Triunto. As we park Lucy in front of the immigration window we are immediately surrounded by a bevy of "facilitators" offering their services, and

*Above: Arenal in Costa Rica, said to be the most active volcano in the world. Left: Visit from an iguana at our camp in La Tigra National Park, Honduras.*

by money-changers offering to exchange US dollars for córdobas, the Nicaraguan currency. All of them talk at us, or rather harangue us vociferously, trying to convince us that crossing the border is impossible without their professional help. We emerge from Lucy and refuse their offers politely but firmly. However, the immigration procedure does indeed prove to be extremely abstruse. But after one and a half hours in scorching heat we've completed the process.

Nicaragua's era of armed conflict, the bitter civil war waged by the Sandinistas first against the Somoza regime and then against the Contras, is long past. Yet there are signs that the country has not yet recovered. After Haiti, Nicaragua is the second poorest country in the Western hemisphere. The road is in an appalling state. Seventy percent of Nicaragua's population live below the poverty line, and thirty percent are considered to suffer from malnutrition.

We spend the night in the old colonial city of León, taking a hotel room with a view of the old quarter and the cathedral. León was the capital of Nicaragua for over 200 years and is regarded as the country's revolutionary stronghold. Its streets are roughly cobbled; its colonial facades reveal the prosperity of times past. To-

day the plaster is crumbling from the walls and the lanes are strewn with potholes as big as craters. The city is like an old book with a fascinating story to tell, but whose pages are yellowed into illegibility. We stroll along bustling streets, examine the 18th century cathedral and watch the crowds at the utilitarian Parque Central. But the oppressive, humid heat of the dusty city paralyzes us. We abandon our plans to stay longer and leave León the next morning.

After the provincial capital of Riva, we head west and, after 20 kilometers (66 feet) of bouncing and jolting, arrive at the little town of San Juan del Sur on the Pacific shore. The glorious Pacific coast is our home for two nights, as we snorkel, swim, fish in the ocean and explore the area's extensive beaches. On the second night, thieves sneak into our wild camp and make off with some towels from the line and three (!) pairs of my shoes. And that makes me really mad. They're shoes that are difficult or even impossible to find in this part of the world (where the heck should I start looking for size 45 Birkenstocks in Nicaragua?). More seriously, the thought that someone was sneaking around our camp at night without our noticing leaves us feeling sick to our stomachs. We pack up and head for Costa Rica.

It's all true: Costa Rica is different from its Central American neighbors – a star student in a class of ruffians, you could say. The country is relatively prosperous and its population has the highest standard of living in Central America, with free schooling and healthcare. Costa Rica disbanded its army in 1949 and enjoys a stable democracy. "Ticos," as its inhabitants are known, are regarded as progressive and eco-conscious. Their philosophy of life can be summed up as "pura vida" – life pure and simple. There are two border crossings between Nicaragua and Costa Rica; we head for the larger of the two at Peñas Blancas, and are absolutely thunderstruck. Fourteen (!) officials take up our case one after the other, and it takes us three hours to collect all the stamps and papers we need. We head south along a poorly surfaced road and search for a grocery store in the little town of Liberia to stock up on provisions – but we end up in a food palace that clearly demonstrates

*Snorkeling, swimming, fishing ...*

*Above, right and opposite page: We hike all day through Monteverde's mountain cloud forests, spotting thumb-size frogs, acrobatic howler monkeys and quetzals, the sacred birds*

how prosperous the country is, crammed with fine cheeses and sausage, wholegrain bread, Nivea shower gel, sushi snacks for lunch. Awesome! Near Puntarenas we turn to the east and toil up a rough road, climbing to altitudes of up to 1,800 meters (5,904 feet). The rain has turned parts of the track into a mudslide, and we take the last 25 kilometers (15 miles) in first gear with four-wheel drive, arriving at the hamlet of Monteverde in the fog and finding a spot in the garden of a little lodge.

After a pleasantly cool night we pack a rucksack the next morning, don rain gear and sturdy boots and set off to hike in the mountain cloud forests of Reserva Monteverde. We enter a riotously lush primeval world of breathtaking beauty. A narrow, slushy path leads through the musty undergrowth, penetrated only by occasional shafts of daylight. The plants low on the forest floor – ferns, mosses and herbs – have frugal needs. A sizeable troop of industrious leaf-cutter ants marching along a well-trodden channel crosses our path, which gradually as-

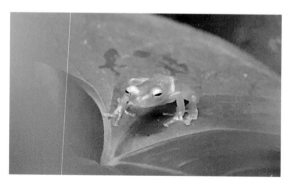

cends to mist-wreathed heights. Unfamiliar birdsong accompanies us – perhaps we will get to see a quetzal after all? Quetzals nest in trees at the lower canopy level of tropical forests, where orchids and bromeliads grow on creeper-entwined tree trunks and collect water in their funnel-shaped leaf bases. As dead insects and leaves fall into these tiny "ponds," a miniature biotope gradually develops, benefiting numerous fauna such as salamander and frogs. Rain begins to patter down – or is it fog condensing in the leaves of the forest canopy? The dense foliage

around thirty meters (98 feet) above the ground arches over us like the vault of a temple. Since the floor of virgin forests is low in nutrients and larger trees cannot develop deep root systems in the ground, their roots spread out to form enormous shelves. We cross a deep gorge over a swaying suspension bridge and again begin to ascend. Finally, between the lush foliage and the mighty trees, we spot it – a Resplendant Quetzal! And it's not alone; a couple are perching in the branches a little way apart and seem to be entertaining each other with a concert of trilling song. They're so beautiful! Both are clothed in iridescent green feathers which merge into a blue tinge towards the back, but only the male has the magnificent tail feathers up to one meter (3,28 feet) long which earned the quetzal the name of "sacred bird" from the Mayans and Aztecs. The quetzals perch motionless on their branches, giving us plenty of time to scrutinize them through our binoculars. Quetzals are rare today, and their habitats are limited to inaccessible mountain forests and reserves.

The sight of these lovely birds still moves the human soul. When the pair eventually flies on, flashing us a glimpse of the red feathers on their undersides, we have the feeling that a further chapter of our journey has closed.

In the evening we sit at Lucy's side wrapped in blankets, eating pasta with canned tuna, drinking tea and smoking a couple of cigarettes. Our day spent in Monteverde's mountain cloud forests has removed all desire to make conversation. I recall a quotation from Albrecht Dürer that I found in a guidebook: "If you seek to know true beauty, go out into the natural world, and there you shall find it."

Next day, Lucy groans down a miserable track towards Lago Arenal, the largest lake in Costa Rica. We somehow get the impression that road building is not Costa Rica's strong point, as we bounce from one crater-deep pothole to the next, the cab rocking ominously from side to side. On the south-eastern arm of

*Chilling at the Caribbean*

In the heart of Costa Rica: Tom's Café

*Top and opposite page: Lush, verdant nature in the forests around La Fortunas, Costa Rica.*

Lago Arenal towers one of the world's most active volcanoes, Arenal. Since it covered several square kilometers with lava, rocks and ashes in 1968, the mountain has never been quiet. Lava regularly flows down the slopes into the valley, warns our guidebook; "several eruptions per day may occur, and at night the orange glow of volcanic rock illuminates the sky." It would be nice, but the mountain has been hiding bashfully behind a curtain of gray rain clouds for days. We stay around Arenal for three nights, hiking through lush rainforests and descending into deep gorges where mighty waterfalls thunder – but we never do manage to see the top of the mountain.

We decide not to approach Panama directly, but permit ourselves another detour down to the Caribbean coast where the rainforests extend to the shore. After all, we've now been on the road

for a year, and we think we're entitled to a short break. To the south of the Caribbean town of Puerto Viejo we rent a comfortable house on the beach, set in tropical gardens, and simply enjoy ourselves – practicing "pura vida." Afternoons are spent lazing in the hammock on the veranda, Sabine painting watercolors as I edit photographs. Occasionally we swim in the warm ocean and cook princely feasts in the evenings on our five (!) burner stove. At night, we stretch out in two (!) kingsize beds swathed in mosquito nets and listen to the Caribbean breakers on the shore, the crickets chirping in the gardens, monkeys howling in the trees and the tropical rain hammering on the tin roof. On Friday, July 9 we are sitting in a little beach bar in Puerto Viejo, the only Germans there watching the opening game of the World Cup – Germany against Costa Rica. Germany wins 4:2 and the people around us join our celebrations. Yes, we've got the hang of "pura vida!"

# Panama – Colombia: The wild jungles of bureaucracy

*"When you arrive in a foreign country, bow your head, even if the place is unaccustomed."*

*Orides Fontela, Brazilian poet*

[km/miles 39,997/23,998 to 42,409/25,445|
Puerto Viejo – Ipiales]

In Colombia, long stretches of the Panamericana are smoothly tarred.

Let's take a long-overdue excursion into American history: On December 23, 1936, at the Inter-American Conference for the Maintenance of Peace in Buenos Aires, a treaty was signed which envisaged the construction of a single highway running through the entire double continent of America. This occasion was the birth of the Pan-American Highway, or, to give the highway its Spanish name, Carretera Panamericana – a more mellifluous title for Central European ears. Since those times enormous efforts have been made to realize the plan, and the Panamericana highway system now extends for an impressive 48,000 kilometers (29,400 miles), crossing fourteen states on its way. The highway is now navigable by car throughout its length from Fairbanks/Alaska to Ushuaia/Tierra del Fuego, with only a tiny ninety-kilometer (295 feet) stretch between Panama and Colombia required to complete it. The mountainous virgin forest of Darien Gap conceals guerrillas, drug-smugglers and poisonous snakes – but no road. We have to ship Lucy to South America.

The little border crossing of Sixaola on the Caribbean coast between Costa Rica and Panama is as isolated as it is sleepy. We reach it around midday and are processed swiftly on the Costa Rican side; however, on the Panama side it's no go – closed for lunch. In the no-man's

land between the borders, we park Lucy in front of a little café. The sociable owner is keen to show off his knowledge of German in front of his handful of guests. However, his language skills are confined to the two words "alles klar"(Sure!). Well, what the heck – that's plenty for a lively conversation. Us (in Spanish, mind you): "May we park here?" "Alles klar!" "Coffee with milk, please!" – "Alles klar!" "Where's the restroom?" – "Alles klar!" – "What time does the crossing open again?" – "Alles klar!" Great! Half an hour and one poured-away coffee later, we're standing before the desk of a heavily made-up woman border official, who stamps our entry papers in the wink of an eye. Bienvenido to Panama!

Panama is a small country, writhing like a snake between the two Americas and no more than 178 kilometers (107 miles) wide from east to west. We reach Panama City the next day, an urban melting-pot prostrate in the paralyzing tropical heat. We have never experienced a more dramatic confrontation of bitter poverty and prosperous luxury. The skyline could easily compete with a US metropolis, the Panama Canal floods the city's coffers with dollars and liberal banking laws attract foreign investment, but distribution of wealth is not on the agenda; between skyscrapers, shopping malls and car

showrooms, bedraggled people huddle in pitiful desolation. Balboa yacht club is tipped in the travel scene as a safe meeting and starting point for the upcoming process of shipping to Colombia. And indeed, we park Lucy next to four other vans from Europe: Christina and Bausi from Switzerland in their Mitsubishi (Wolf), Harald and Petra in a Land Cruiser (Toddel), Nils, Anke and daughter Maya (aged 2) in "Goldie", their Volkswagen Transporter, and Haye and Willeke from the Netherlands, also in a Land Cruiser called "Bruce" (travelers are crazy; they give their cars pet-names and wear khaki shirts!). In the evening we sit in the yacht club's open-air bar, sipping cold Balboa beer and exchanging tips and experiences, bringing ourselves up-to-date on all we need to know about shipping.

During this time, Barwil shipping agency seems to be the most reliable address in Panama, arranging container, ro/ro and lo/lo transport to Colombia (in the latter, the freight is loaded onto the ship by crane). Next day, nine of us throng into the air-conditioned chill of Evelyn Batista's office. She is a genial member of the Barwil team, with broad hips and charmingly accented English. Suitable container transport for all the vehicles is found relatively quickly at a remarkably low price – all except for Lucy, that is; she's too high to fit into a normal container. Evelyn promises to arrange an open-top container, evidently optimistic that one can be found by the end of the week, and sends us and the others off to embark on a complex, time-consuming battle with red tape. We go to the customs office the same afternoon to have our

import papers corrected because there are errors in Lucy's and Wolf's documents. In our case the vehicle chassis number and my name are incorrect, with "Name of Owner" given as "Michael Boyny Herr" – quite enough to cause insurmountable confusion among the officials here. We ask for new papers to be issued.

Next morning the whole group of us turns up at "Policia Tecnica Judicial," where our vehicles are compared with the (corrected) documents and we receive confirmation that we are the due owners of same and have not been involved in any accidents in the last eight days. It's a tedious procedure; one grumpy police officer toils away at a pre-war computer and doesn't notice that the printer is on the blink until after having processed the third vehicle. Of course none of the forms the policeman had previously completed were saved in any way, so he simply starts all over again. Hours later, we're led across the street to a new administration building where our newly printed forms are handed in to a receptionist. Once again we sit in a waiting-room and kill time until some in-

"Team talk."

visible functionary signs a new form for us to present to customs later. But this waiting-room has a TV showing the Germany – Ecuador game. The functionary can take all the time he wants …!

Armed with all the necessary documents, we trek to the customs office in the afternoon. I have no idea what papers we have to apply for here, but in any case it takes hours before we finally collect them and at long last have all the documents we need for shipping. Now all Lucy needs is a ship! That evening, the whole crew of us stakes out Evelyn's office once more. Everyone hands over their documents, as proud as school kids showing off straight A report cards – only Sabine and I are greeted with bad news; an open-top container has been found, but the carrier can't agree with Barwil Agency over the price.

Next morning I call Evelyn as agreed, only to find that no agreement has been reached and I should call again in the afternoon. Hours later, I do – and find that still no progress has been made. "OK, Evelyn," I tell her, "I'll be at your office in twenty minutes and we'll look for a new solution." I unload the scooter from its platform and race over to Barwil through streets choked with Panama City's rush-hour traffic. In the office, Evelyn and I sit at the computer perched

on her cluttered desk and examine all the options. She telephones a few carriers, writes e-mails and consults her boss. Finally our persistence is rewarded: the "Westerhaven" will leave Colón in three days' time and arrive at Cartagena the following day. A platform has been reserved for Lucy, on which she will be winched onto the ship. Our jaunt will cost us 1,950 US dollars, around twenty percent more than it cost us to ship Lucy all the way from Germany to Canada.

The next day, shortly after sunrise, five European camper vans set out on the eighty-kilometer (48 miles) journey to Colón. "Lonely Planet" has this to say about the port on the Caribbean coast: "Warning! Colón is a dangerous slum. Do yourself a favor and avoid it unless your journey is really essential. Crime is a serious problem. It is not only possible but probable that you will be mugged, even in the daytime. If you have to move around Colón take a taxi and don't even think of walking."

There are two harbors in the town. Bruce, Toddel, Wolf and Goldie are booked into Manzania, while we head for Puerto Cristóbal. At the harbor, the process of handover is completed in a pleasantly speedy three hours. New customs and freight papers are issued, we pay harbor fees and Lucy is inspected one last time before we have to abandon her in a dusty parking lot between containers and rolls of metal plate – a parting tinged with emotion. To avoid any risk, we follow Lonely Planet's suggestions to the letter and beyond, hop into a taxi and are driven the eighty kilometers (48 miles) back to Panama City. After all, what's an extra forty dollars at this stage?

The next day, a Saturday, the aircraft of the Panamanian airline COPA gently – and punctually – touches down on the runway at Cartageñas. Our first time on South American soil! And I must say it's a pretty wet place: tropical downpours have flooded the streets of the old colonial city. Finding a hotel in the city center is a laborious process; it's not easy to accommodate ten travelers, all with different ideas about standards of comfort and varying budgets. But we want to bring our story to its end togeth-

*Opposite page: Colombian tempta- tion – sweet fruit for sale in the streets of Cartageña. Left: Delightful, perpetually friendly people.*

er, so at least eight out of ten agree to the pretty Hotel Villa Colonia in a narrow lane in the old quarter. We take advantage of the long weekend – Monday is a Colombian holiday – for long strolls through Cartageña's beautiful old quarter, where magnificent colonial buildings line bustling squares, street traders sell exquisite crafts and performance groups dance passionately to the Afro-Caribbean rhythms of the drums.

The people are friendly and helpful, and the lively, carefree bustle of the lanes captivates us. It's hard to believe that we're in a country classified as "dangerous" by the German Foreign Office, which discourages travelers from coming here. The only criminal elements we encounter in these enjoyable days are the high temperatures and unbearable humidity. But on Tuesday the party's over, and we prepare to free our vehicles from the claws of the harbor. The container clique heads off in a body to the container port, while Sabine and I once again have a different destination. Fearing the process here could be even more complicated than in Panama, we ask Daniela, the eighteen-year-old

Bodyguard

*Secure terrain in the wild mountains north of Medellín, Colombia.*

daughter of the hotel owner, to accompany us as our interpreter. She speaks wonderful English and proves over the next two days to be a highly professional agent. Finally, after twelve taxi rides through Cartageña, thirty-seven photocopies, 298 US dollars in costs and fees (not including the taxi rides), around eighteen different officials, two chewed fingernails and around a trillion irreparably damaged nerve cells, we can finally steer Lucy through the port barriers into the streets of Cartageña. If inefficiency is a cardinal virtue, the entire staff of the Colombian and Panamanian customs offices should be canonized!

For reasons of safety, we travel south in a convoy with Haye, Willeke, Nils, Anke and little Maya along the Panamericana through neat and tidy Colombia. We traverse dramatic mountain scenery with coffee plantations hugging the slopes and drive through friendly villages where the inhabitants greet us cheerfully. There is strong military and police presence along the whole route, and the roads are in excellent condition. Wherever we stop, we do so at checkpoints where obliging uniformed staff always have time for a chat. Many people we met on our journey advised us to avoid the country because it is too dangerous; however, in reality the guerrillas and paramilitaries have left tourists in peace for years, unless one of them happens to stumble across a coca field.

In the little mountain village of Silvia we visit the weekly market. Indigenous rural farmers from the Guambia tribe throng in from the surrounding countryside in colorful buses to sell vegetables, fruit, livestock and tools, wearing traditional costumes of thick hand-woven fabric and black felt hats.

Because tourists are rare, the place has a more authentic, genuine atmosphere than anything comparable that we encountered in Central America. Here, there are no traders eager to

tap the lucrative souvenir market, no begging children scrambling after us and clamoring for a few pesos; instead we meet shy, courteous people who view my camera with distrust and sell us local vegetables at a fair price. Here, we're at the heart of a world which, we always believed, was no more than a sanitized shadow of itself on the National Geographic channel.

We spend our last night before leaving for Ecuador at a pleasantly cool altitude of 1,800 meters, (5904 feet) at a real campground with showers, toilets and electricity. All around us the mountains tower to over 5,000 meters (16,400 feet), and next to our camp a stream tumbles down into the valley. Children from a school trip creep inquisitively around our vehicles, the bravest greeting us with a shy "buenos días." Mauricio, the campground owner, has set up a TV under a canopy for us to watch the World Cup final of Italy against France. The second half is about to start. I fetch a cold "Club Columbia" from Carlos at the kiosk and join the others.

*Above: Livestock transport the Colombian way at Silvia market.*
*Left: Indigenous farming women from the Guambia people in traditional costume.*

# Ecuador: Free the Cuy!

"Travel leads to encounters with others, which always presents an opportunity to encounter oneself."
Luis Sepúlveda, Chilean author

[km/miles 42,409/25,445 to 44,829/26,897|
Ipiales – Vilcabamba]

Goatherd in the Andes near Zumbahua, Ecuador.

Yet another border crossing, our fourteenth so far. Initially a reason for tremendous excitement, by now they're nothing more than tedious routine. Between Colombia and Ecuador the procedure is familiar: get an emigration stamp on the Colombian side of border, hand in customs papers for Lucy, get an immigration stamp in Ecuador, have import papers issued for Lucy and the scooter. The whole process takes a laborious three and a half hours! But a new factor is the altitude at which we now move from country to country: at just under 3,000 meters (9840 feet), the border town of Ipiales is quite a change. And we just keep going up and up. The Panamericana serpentines its way up to a lofty 3,400 meters (11,152 feet), past volcanoes almost 6,000 meters (19,680 feet) in height, and slashes through a region of towering mountains which will accompany us through the next months on our way south – the Andes. The longest mountain chain in the world runs from Venezuela to Patagonia and is, in a way, also the highest. Let me explain. Thanks to the earth's equatorial bulge, 6,267-meter (20,556 feet) Mount Chimborazo here in Ecuador is actually 2,152 meters (7,059 feet) further from the center of the earth than Mount Everest!

In the little town of Otavalo we (the group still includes Nils and Anke with little Maya, their daughter, Haye and Willeke, Sabine and me) and our three RVs find a spot for the night in the parking lot of a beautiful hacienda. We've now been on the road as a convoy for three weeks, by this stage less for reasons of safety than because the seven of us have fallen into an easy, pleasant rhythm of traveling together. On the road we all head off at our own speeds and quickly lose sight of each other, but at the end of the day we always manage to meet up again, set up camp together and take it in turns to cook and eat, pushing our folding tables together to form one large one. Even a night parking lot at a gas station, a place of limited charms, loses something of its gray asphalt cheerlessness in this sociable group.

Otavalo is famous beyond the borders of Ecuador for its crafts market. In the town and its surrounding villages, indigenas weave gorgeous fabrics and sell them on the Plaza de los Ponchos as blankets, carpets, scarves and ... well, of course, as ponchos. The "otavaleños" favor traditional costume; the women wear ornamented blouses, long black shirts, shawls knotted at the side and folded scarves on their heads, while men wear stiffly creased calf-length white pants and ponchos, with bowler hats over their braided hair. The market attracts busloads of tourists ferried in on day trips from Quito, Ecuador's capital, and the range of goods on offer has shifted to take the preferences of these tourists into consideration. Prices are seductively low, and at the end of the day we return to our vehicles

with crammed shopping bags. This evening we seven hold a farewell celebration with a delicious dinner, wine and tequila, before tomorrow's parting of the ways for Lucy, Bruce and Goldie. We've grown fond of each other on this joint route between Panama and Ecuador, and

even if our friendship won't continue all the way down to Ushuaia, there are still tears shed tonight.

The journey to Quito is less than a hundred kilometers (60 miles), during which we cross the equator – but unfortunately we fail to notice it. Sabine and I are so deep in conversation that we only realize 20 kilometers (12 miles) after the fact that we've just crossed the most famous line in the world. Quito – a city with a population of one million – lies at a breathless altitude of 2,800 meters (9,184 feet). We toil through busy streets into the colonial old town, a designated World Heritage site, and rent a room in "Real Audencia" Hotel on Plaza Santo Domingo, overlooking the ancient square on whose southeastern side the towers of the 17th century church of Santo Domingo rise. The view makes up for the din of traffic throughout the night

Above: Otavaleñas in their richly ornamented traditional costumes.
Left: Livestock dealers and farmers haggle over prices on market day in Zumbahua.

*Above: Sea of houses in the thin air – Quito, 2,800 meters (9,184 feet) above sea level. Right: Fountain in front of San Francisco church in Quito's old quarter.*

and for the dreadful coffee at breakfast. In 1526 the Spanish came to this volcano-fringed valley and founded the city on the ruins of an old Inca settlement. Within a few decades, fired by missionary zeal, they established magnificent churches and monasteries in order to remove all doubt about just which divinity would hold sway over the natives in future. Their majestic cathedrals were built with Inca sweat, and their glorious altars decorated with Inca gold. It's the same tragic story which has dogged us since Mexico: a story of the destruction, displacement and oppression of a centuries-old civilization, coupled with the simultaneous establishment of a Catholic culture which appears to be even more resplendent and ostentatious than that of old Europe. We stroll through museums, churches and monasteries, sit on Baroque steps and watch the bustling crowds on attractive squares where smartly dressed businessmen in suits and ties are glued to their mobile phones as street children shine their shoes for a few centavos.

Children clean shoes with their bare hands on Plaza de San Francisco for a few centavos.

Hunched indigenas beg the hurrying tourists for a few coppers, while smitten young mestizos canoodle on the steps of monumental fountains.

We're strolling by daylight through a quiet side street in the district of Mariscal when two sinister guys approach us. I don't take any notice of them until Sabine informs me that they're coming towards us with knives. Indeed, the taller one is holding an open box cutter while the other menaces us by flashing a kitchen knife with a five-inch blade. "Give me money," he snarls as he lurches towards us. Now as everyone knows it's unwise to play the hero in a situation like this, but in this case, what we're facing is a pair of pint-sized dummies. One is limping heavily over the cobblestones, while the other's hand holding the knife is swathed in bandages – surely any Central European guy worth his salt should be able to give these guys a run for their money. I draw myself up to my full height and let rip, bellowing at them – in English, which is a sign of authority in these parts: "Get out of my way, you fucking idiots!" I roar. "Who the hell do you think you are? You looking for trouble?" One of them skedaddles immediately, while the other adopts his menacing air once more and

flourishes his potato-peeling knife. That does it. Furious, I'm about to slam our "Footprint" guidebook down on his head (1,572 pages, weighs a ton), but Sabine holds me back and the guy beats it. It all sounds so harmless after the event, but the shock sits deep in our bones. We take each other by the arm, march straight back to the busy Avenida Amazonas, where we feel safer, and decide to leave the city the same day. Quito, we're outta here!

From Quito we drive 55 kilometers (33 miles) down the Panamericana to the highest active volcano in the world, snow-capped Cotopaxi. A rough, endlessly spiraling dirt track leads up to the foot of the volcano at an altitude of around 4,000 meters (13,120 feet). We spend the night by a shallow lagoon in the midst of a dramatic landscape. Hiding bashfully behind thick cloud at first, by the late afternoon Cotopaxi gradually starts to emerge, flashing broad, stony hips, then snow-covered shoulders; finally, just before the sun touches the horizon, we see the mountain revealed in all its glory. I'm absolutely certain that this mountain

Ninety-five percent of all Ecuadorians are Catholics

*Cotopaxi, the highest active volcano in the world with a height of 5,897 meters (19,342 feet), gradually reveals itself*

*Camp fire at 3,000 meters (9,840 feet) above sea level*

is a woman, and I know I've just seen the most exciting striptease in my life! Our night at 4,000 meters (13,120 feet) is freezing cold; it's hard to believe that we're at the equator. At this height the air has only half as much oxygen as at sea level, making our breathing labored and sleep elusive.

We travel west of the Panamericana and, after a laborious journey over steep mountain passes, we finally arrive at the isolated Indio village of Zumbahua. It's Friday; on Saturdays the indigena from the surrounding regions come into town with their llamas and buy and sell vegetables and meat at the simple market. We find a parking spot for the night in the garden of a homely country hotel not far from the nearby crater lake of Quilotoa, and spend the evening in the hotel's heated restaurant eating a three-course meal of regional delicacies at seven euros per person. The main course is "cuy," grilled domestic guinea-pig, which has been considered a

delicacy by Ecuador's highland Indians for the past 5,000 years. It's accompanied by "mote," boiled corn and onion sauce. We find the bony meat is a tough problem, but our biggest issue is with the local way of serving it; the poor animal lies on the plate whole, its four paws spread, the dead eye sockets staring accusingly at us and two pointed incisors seemingly poised to nibble at our corn. A culinary chamber of horrors.

The next morning we stroll through Zumbahua's market. The indigena here make a brusquer impression than those in Otavalo further north; their traditional costume is plain and unornamented, and they speak an unfamiliar language to each other, probably Quechua, the national language of the ancient Inca Empire. They greet us with reserve or at best surprise, and generally refuse my request to take photos. Many of the men get drunk in tiny bars dotted around the marketplace while their wives appear to take care of business. Children with grubby faces romp around between the stalls, stopping short in confusion when they en-

counter us. We love the atmosphere of this archaic bustle around us, and yet we feel like unwelcome intruders, worlds away from bustling Quito or touristy Otavalo where the people are poorer, but less focused on outsiders. We soon decide to leave Zumbahua.

In the little village of Vilcabamba in the far south of the country, we're temporarily enchanted by an idyllic spot and stay for the time being with German brothers Dieter and Peter at their "Hostal Izcayluma." The property sits on a slope above the village, set amid a lush tropical garden. If the mountain further to the north was steep, bare and rugged – typically male – here on its eastern flank it is softer, more sensuous: female. The mild temperatures and relatively low altitudes do us good. We pamper ourselves with massages and reiki sessions and enjoy the finest of German home cooking, with a plate of Koenigsberg-style meatballs on the first evening – a dish I haven't eaten since my childhood. It tastes delicious – a far cry from "cuy" … and anyway, free the guinea-pigs!

Top: Quilotoa crater lake near the mountain village of Zumbahua, Ecuador.
Left: Hottest hat fashions in Vilcabamba.

# Galapagos

In the middle of the Pacific, around 1,000 kilometers (600 miles) off the coast of Ecuador, Planet Earth set up its experimental site and tested evolution on the Galapagos archipelago. Here, on the islands' 7,882 square meters (25,853 feet), the history of creation unfolds like a picture-book. In the beginning, submarine volcanoes belched great streams of magma to the surface of the sea, where it hardened into bizarre formations of cones and slabs. Eventually the crusted surface became colonized by sparse vegetation, perhaps brought here in the feathers and droppings of the birds which discovered ideal nesting places among the black basalt cliffs. They were followed by reptiles, floating out on tree trunks and branches into the calm ocean from their home on the continental coast to land in the isolated lava world. Life in this hostile seclusion required extreme abilities to adapt, and over the course of millions of years natural selection generated new species and subspecies. With no natural enemies and rivals, the animals on the islands had no need of fear, and never developed the instinct of flight. Today, careless visitors run the risk of trampling a sunbathing lizard or broody bird every few steps.

Our cabin on the "Estrella del Mare"

We spend a week exploring these island worlds on the "Estrella del Mare," where we occupy a small double cabin with shower on the second deck. The boat has eight cabins on board, and the sixteen tour guests are tended around the clock by the seven-strong crew. Meals are served three times a day; two cooks busy themselves in a kitchen offering only a little more space than Lucy's tiny kitchenette, and still produce decent food. Although after a few days we start to suffer from classic "canteen syndrome" and have the impression that everything tastes exactly the same – prawns, chocolate cake, chicken, fruit salad, tomato soup – our predecessors' warnings that we would never feel replete prove to be untrue. Billy, our guide, is an old hand where the Galapagos are concerned,

lacking neither comprehensive knowledge of biology and geography nor self-confidence. He is utterly charming, and occasionally utterly bored. English, Americans, Israelis, Swiss and Germans share the cramped ship – and everything works out just fine. In the evenings, after a long day, we sit together in the bar of the "Estrella del Mare," play cards or chat about blue-footed boobies, snorkeling techniques or recipes – by tacit agreement, political topics are excluded from discussion. A day on the Galapagos begins early. After a rough night on the Pacific waves, where we sleep like babies thanks to a dose of highly effective seasickness remedy, we are already at the breakfast table at seven. The scrambled eggs taste pretty similar to yesterday's pasta... Forty-five minutes later we climb into a dinghy with outboard motor and head for one of the islands. Each island reveals its own surprises; on North Seymore we spot frigate birds and blue-footed boobies. In the mating season, the male frigate bird inflates its bright red throat pouch to impress females; blue-footed boobies proudly flaunt their blue flippers for the same purpose, stretching their necks and waddling as if in slow motion from left to right. Fortunately the female blue-footed boobies are impressed by this dance, while frigate bird females are crazy about inflated gular pouches – so the populations of both species are regarded as stable. South Plaza Island is a tiny islet just big enough to serve as the habitat of its own species of land iguana. Over one meter (3 feet) long, these iguanas are endemic to the island and are found only here. A count has shown their population to be around 500, and we see five of them in an hour – that's one percent of the world's entire population. Isla Española is the nesting-site for Galapagos albatross. The largest birds on the archipelago with a wingspan of up to 2.4 meters (8 feet), they spend months on the open sea without ever touching land, but return to this very island to breed – here and only here; they have never been sighted anywhere else in the archipelago or otherwise. We spot pelicans and cormorants, penguins, finches and the brightly colored "Sally Lightfoot" crab. And then there are the omnipresent sea iguanas, the only species of lizard in the world to have adopted an amphibian lifestyle. They spread-eagle themselves motionless on the black rocks to regain their high body temperature after long dives. At midday we return to the "Estrella" for a three-course meal and then sleep it off in a long siesta before exploring more islands or snorkeling in the afternoon. The sea is pretty cold, thanks to the Humboldt current flowing from Antarctic regions, and we wear wetsuits when we snorkel. We encounter sea-lions everywhere, snoozing on the broad beaches after a night of hunting; in the water, however, they come ominously close to us and frolic with us high-spiritedly, shooting up at us from the depths only to twist away at the last minute and dive underneath us. At first we are thoroughly scared by these playful attacks, but then we get into the spirit and try in vain to keep up. Occasionally we spot reef sharks – another reason to be worried; but they're harmless and don't even notice us.

Of course, we weren't the first to set foot on the Galapagos. Charles Darwin arrived at the islands in 1835 during his world travels, and stayed there for five weeks studying the fauna and making copious notes. His observations would later form the basis of his theory of evolution, according to which all living creatures – including human beings – evolved from the same origins and adapted in response to the conditions of their environment. It was thanks to adaptation and selection, then, that Galapagos land lizards are able to swim while Galapagos cormorants are unable to fly. Makes sense. However, exactly what evolution had in mind when it came up with the giant turtle is a complete mystery. These creatures seem to have developed from a caprice of nature, some mammoth attempt to unite everything that's useless and ridiculous

A gaggle of explorers: tour guests on the Galapagos

in a single being. And so today the giant turtle, weighing anything up to 150 kilograms, drags its heavy, lumpy body around through the pampas on tiny, weirdly twisted stumpy legs. Nature also failed to give the poor creature adequate undercarriage clearance, so that it runs aground on every rock, flapping feebly to and fro until gravity takes pity and it plummets to the ground. The mighty shell which the giant turtle drags around on its back also seems futile in a world devoid of natural enemies – if we discount man. But despite these objections, the giant turtle is the star of the Galapagos, even lending the archipelago its name: "galapago" means turtle.

At sunset we return exhausted to the "Estrella del Mare," with just enough time for a cold shower before we're called to dinner. Afterwards, before going to bed, we chat with John from Oregon at the bar about river tours of the Amazon, or to Nadav from Israel about hiking in Nepal – all travelers together, over a beer which confusingly enough tastes not dissimilar to this morning's breakfast coffee. Evolution may have generated an infinite variety, both here on the Galapagos and the rest of the planet – but it omitted the cuisine on the "Estrella del Mare."

Frigate bird off South Plaza Island.

Whatever turns you on: frigate bird with inflated throat pouch.

Thousands of sealions inhabit the archipelago.

The giant turtle that gave the islands their name.

Albatross on Isla Española.

Star of the Galapagos: the blue-footed booby.

The omnipresent Sally Lightfoot crab.

Sea iguanas have adapted to an amphibian life.

Galapagos archipelago, Ecuador

ECUADOR
Vilcabamba
Punta
Aguja
Chiclayo
Trujillo
PAZIFIC OCEAN
PERU
Lima
Huancayo
Nasca
0    180 miles
0    300 km

# The Coast of Peru: Dark Days

*"Travel requires patience, courage, humor and the ability not to be dispirited by minor adversities."*
*Freiherr Adolph von Knigge (1752–96)*

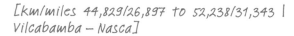

[km/miles 44,829/26,897 to 52,238/31,343 | Vilcabamba – Nasca]

*At the Peruvian border we toil through the dense jungle along near-impassable tracks.*

Off to Peru. Three border crossings connect Ecuador with its neighbor to the south: Tumbes on the coast, Macará in the central upland, and La Chonta. The latter is so small, so isolated and unknown that even the inhabitants of Loja (the last large city we pass through in Ecuador) at the gas station are convinced it doesn't exist. We prefer to trust our "Footprint": if it's good enough to scare off knife-toting muggers, it can't be far off the mark as a reliable source of information!

Initially tarred but bumpy, the road to the south undulates gently through the contemplative Andean highlands. It's an ideal washday route – but let me explain. Our washing machine, you see, is nothing more than a 25-liter water canister with a wide, sealable opening. We fill it with dirty laundry, add detergent, fill the canister up with water and let it swish around on its own as we drive. At the end of the day we rinse out the washing and hang it up on a line, and that's it. Soon the road narrows to a single-lane track. We leave the last tilled fields behind and plunge into lush, humid jungle territory. At altitudes above 2,000 meters (6560 feet) the highlands are shrouded in mist and the track becomes muddy and slippery. Our progress is slow and laborious, taking almost six hours to reach the border crossing (which does exist) only a little over 110 kilometers (66 miles) away.

The Río Calvas forms the boundary line between Ecuador and Peru. Formalities are completed with surprising speed and friendliness. On the Peru side the condition of the track improves slightly. We pass unimposing settlements or simple mud huts standing alone, aware that we are being scrutinized from open doorways and holes in the mud walls. In the unremarkable little town of San Ignazio, two hours south of the border, we exchange dollars for the Peruvian currency of soles in a general store, buy some fruit and vegetables and make for Jaén and a secure parking spot at a 24-hour gas station.

From Jaén we finally reach the Pacific coast, a day's journey away. After the primeval tropical world on the eastern flank of the Andes we are now at sea level, our movements as if on another planet. We drive through a dismal desert, a barren expanse of scree under a heavily overcast sky before a gray ocean. The Humboldt current off the coast cools down the warm Pacific air and condenses it into fog which moves inland. But the low humidity is insufficient to cause any significant rainfall, so that the coast is as gray as it is dry as it is – in many areas – desolate. It seems to affect our mood somehow; it's hard to find any real cheer. For days we head listlessly south, rarely stopping. Is travel-weariness rearing its ugly head after almost 50,000 kilometers (30,000 miles)? Suddenly the things

we used to find exciting are simply irritations. Now, the never-ending inquisitive stares of the Peruvians standing around Lucy in the evenings are over-familiar and tiresome. Bumpy tracks are no longer paths leading to adventure, but an evil that we avoid wherever possible. Faced with centuries-old ruins from pre-Inca ages, our only response is a blasé yawn.

However, that doesn't mean we ignore them. On the edge of Trujillo, for example, we visit the ruins of Chan Chan, once the capital of the Chimu, a people who ruled a large part of the coastal desert from 1000 to 1450 AD; up to 100,000 people lived in the twenty-square-kilometer (12 miles) complex, which was completely enclosed by an adobe wall. Although today little more than a mass of ruins remains, a colossal ceremonial palace has been partially restored, and our plans are to visit it. In a burst of

*Above: The road leads through isolated, impoverished settlements.*
*Left: Encounter with a friendly local in Jaén.*

Above: Along the Peruvian coast, the Panamericana passes through an endless wasteland of scree. Right: Excavated royal grave at Sipán.

activity, we even fork out twenty soles to have a young Peruvian history student guide us through the site. Unfortunately her English is so poor and hard to understand that we probably would-n't be able to tell if she recited the telephone book at us. Anyway, the adobe walls, ten to 12 meters (39 feet) high and 4 to 5 meters (13 to 16 feet) thick, are impressive. All the corners in the complex have angles over or under ninety degrees. Our student guide was unable to ex-plain this to us, however – or we were unable to understand her.

We approach Lima, the capital of Peru with an estimated population of over ten million peo-ple. Lima was long regarded as the most magnif-icent and cultivated city in South America, until earthquakes, mismanagement and corrup-tion caused its facades to crumble. Today, like almost all South America's major cities, Lima threatens to suffocate under the uncontrolled influx of people, primarily indigenous rural pop-

ulations. The city has an inglorious reputation, and lives up to it hours before we even reach its boundaries, as we stick fast in traffic which has no discernible order. The procedure is to hoot as long and loud as possible and just go for it. It's all the more amazing that the police patrols, which at one stage are stopping us every fifteen

The fishermen at Huanchaco still row far out into the icy Pacific in the simple reed boats their ancestors used.

minutes, claim to be able to spot my driving as a breach of traffic laws in this lawless zone. Within a single day we are accused of the following flagrant infringements: overtaking in a no-overtaking zone (2x); exceeding the speed limit (2x); driving without due insurance (1x). And we are always threatened with the same procedure: confiscation of driving license for an indefinite period plus a fine payable at the nearest police station or, alternatively, a fine payable on the spot, whereupon confiscation of my driving license is generously waived. It would be funny if it weren't so darned annoying. Four times we are allowed to drive on after arguing until we're blue in the face. Once we pay out 340 soles – over eighty euros – for exceeding the speed limit. We're sick and tired of Lima before we've even started looking for a hotel. And so we decide on the spot to make a detour around it.

Around 500 kilometers (300 miles) to the south of Lima we arrive at Nazca, on the edge of one of world's most fascinating prehistoric sites, the Nazca Lines. Eight hundred dead straight lines, three hundred geometrical figures (geoglyphs) and seventy oversized figures of animals and plants have been "carved" into the desert floor of the bone-dry pampas. The markings are almost invisible at ground level; the gigantic figures, channels and mysterious outlines can only be made out from a bird's eye view. The most fascinating are the biomorphs, the depictions of animals: a 180-meter-long (590 feet) lizard, for example, or a spiral-tailed spider monkey, a killer whale, a hummingbird and a man with an owl's head. The significance of the mysterious images is uncertain. They were probably produced by a coastal tribe who lived around 200 BC and who have been given the

The water's too cold for us – but not for him ...

name of "Nazca" today. But what purpose did they serve? Were they part of a gigantic astronomical calendar, ritual procession routes or extraterrestrial landing runways, as one Erich von Däniken would have us believe? We find a lovely parking spot for the night opposite the little airfield in the garden of a hotel – but a water pump driven by a diesel engine roars away on a neighboring plot. We wait for it to be switched off at night – but just how naïve can we get?

# The Lowest Point

The next morning we make another short trip into town. Sabine has to call Germany and I want to buy us some bread. We park Lucy on Plaza de Armas. I must explain that normally we never park Lucy just anywhere: we either look for a manned parking lot or pay someone a few soles to guard her. If neither course of action is possible, we at least store all our valuables in the living quarters, equipped with two rugged locks fit for a fortress. In Nasca – of all places – we depart from this principle. We're in a hurry, eager to get away from the dump. It's ten-thirty on a Sunday morning. The square is becoming busier as people come and go in the churches or sit on the benches in the plaza and chat.

Sabine disappears into a public phone center while I ask passers-by for a "panaderia," keeping an eye on Lucy as I do so. At the butcher's I'm given instructions about finding the nearest bakery, half a block down on the left. I can't see Lucy from there, but don't worry because I'll only be two minutes. I'm the only customer in the store. Great! I buy bread for three soles, equivalent to a dollar, and give the young lad ten. Of course he has no change, as usual (another annoying Peruvian habit: stores never, ever, ever have change, not even seven lousy soles!) The boy trots over to the next store to get change. "Be quick, chico, I'm in a hurry," I pray silently. He eventually returns, I snatch the change from his hand and run back to Lucy. Sabine has also just finished her telephone call, and we reach our truck together.

As I go to unlock the driver's door, I notice immediately that someone has tampered with the lock. An icy shiver runs down my spine as I throw open the door. There is a tray between the seats with drink holders and space for guidebooks. I'd left my camera bag there. But now… the shelf is empty!

I tell Sabine that my camera is gone – and then I scream once again, "My camera's gone!" I circle Lucy like a madman, running over to the square and back, speaking to – no, shouting at a man sitting on a bench not 5 meters (16 feet) away from the vehicle, trying to find out whether he noticed anything. But my thoughts are so confused that I can't frame sentences in Spanish. I stammer to myself, lurch across the asphalt, stare up and down the street. Later I will have no recollection of what Sabine was doing in the seconds I spend wandering around. At some point she is standing in front of me and hugs me, takes me in her arms and doesn't let go for a while.

I don't know whether people can comprehend that a camera is far more than a mere tool for a photographer – or at least that's the way it is for me. You could liken it to the antique Stradivarius of a concert violinist, or the favorite knife of a gourmet chef who is convinced he could never cook without it. My camera is a constant and true companion on all my travels, the sound of its shutter as familiar to me as an old song, the dents and scratches on its case tell tales of all we've been through together. If you blindfolded me, I would still be able to set the camera any way I want. It's as familiar to me as if it were an old friend. And now it's gone!

It's common knowledge in Peru that the country's police force is corrupt and passive and that any attempt to get help from them is more likely to create a new problem than solve an existing one. Nevertheless, we ask the way to Nazca's police station and less than fifteen minutes later are sitting in a bare cubicle in front of a shabby desk atop which sits an ancient Adler typewriter. Officer Luis Alberto Flores Pomez is at the typewriter taking down our statement. Pommes (as we'll call him from now on) is not yet thirty-five, but his face is puffy and his manner self-righteous in the way that Peruvian policemen enjoy. He first sends me off to get copies made of my driving license and passport. It's about now that I start to take a hearty dislike to him.

Opposite the police station is a general store with a photocopier. I hurry over the road, and minutes later

Simple houses in the desert sand

No friend and helper of ours

Pommes has the copies on his desk. He asks unhelpful questions and treats Sabine as if she weren't even in the room (that's another thing they enjoy, those Peruvian policemen: contemptuously ignoring women).

Finally he tells me to go to the Banco de la Nación, pay a fee, retain the receipt and come back at five-thirty; in the meantime he and his colleagues will hunt for the camera. But doesn't he need any details about the stolen objects, I ask. No, the description "professional camera equipment" is enough, he assures me.

We tell him where our vehicle is parked and finally return to the hotel at the airfield to set up camp again next to the noisy pump.

In the early afternoon we have a surprise visit from Pommes. He tells me to accompany him on an interrogation tour of some suspects and well-known criminals. We get into his car, an ancient Toyota, and drive to a district of Nazca where ragged creatures vegetate, eking out a pitiful existence. There are no roads, only paths; there are no houses, not even huts. People are living under spindly trees, protected by canopies of tarpaulin, sleeping on heaps of old tires and wearing tattered rags on their emaciated bodies.

We stop when we cannot drive any further. Pommes gets out, draws his pistol from its holster and takes off the safety-catch. Now I start to get nervous. We walk over the rubble and garbage to the camp of an old, toothless man. Pommes asks a few questions and pokes around with his pistol in the man's few possessions: old clothes, a wrecked cell phone, a pair of women's briefs, the hand of a store display dummy. We go on to a place where two figures are sitting around a small fire, utterly spaced out. The stench of feces and garbage is so powerful that I almost have to vomit. Once again Pommes pulls his show, and after a few minutes we move to the next camp, and so on for an hour. What is Pommes doing here, I wonder. These people are so worn out by hunger, alcohol and drugs that none of them would remotely be able to break into a car within seconds and purposefully take the most valuable item within.

I begin to frame the suspicion that what we have here is a corrupt policeman, demonstrating nothing more than the futile act of investigating for the sake of it. But I still haven't grasped his purpose. On the way back to our parking lot Pommes tells me that he will continue to search poor quarters further away, but that his gas tank is empty and whether I could help him out, since after all he's doing this traveling on my behalf. Is that it? Is all his play-acting only about getting a free tank of gas?

In fact, the needle in the gas gauge actually is all the way over to the left. I press one hundred soles, around thirty dollars, into his hand and implore him, with as

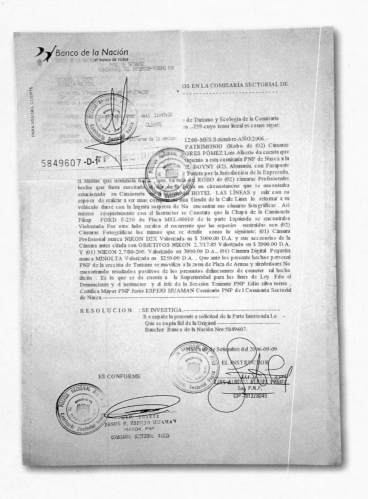

much urgency as my current mood allows me to muster, to do his work well.

One and a half hours later Pommes collects me as agreed and we return to the police station. The needle on the gas gauge is unchanged, but his shoes are different. Previously, after we had marched through the rubble, their black leather had been covered by a layer of gray dust; now they're as shiny as new. The man might have been all over the place, but he certainly hasn't visited any remote poor quarters. At the station Pommes laboriously writes a one-page report. I receive an official copy, accompanied in parting by fatherly advice to continue my travels and leave the work up to the professionals. Pommes slaps me patronizingly on the shoulder and vanishes into a back room, leaving me standing crestfallen. By now it's dark and the desert air has grown significantly cooler.

Tired, frozen and weary, I get into a taxi and return to Sabine. We cook spaghetti and open a bottle of wine, talking little this evening, but deciding to take Pommes' advice and continue the next day to Arequipa. Not because we have any confidence in the professional work of the police, but because this town is making us sick. We withdraw to the cabin like two weary prizefighters, soon turn off the light, cuddle close to each other, stare into the darkness and listen to the throb of the diesel engine around the corner.

Next morning we book an air tour of the mysterious lines for the late afternoon. Around midday we take a taxi to Plaza de Armas, the town's main square. Nazca is a collection of unadorned houses and ruins carelessly flung down in the desert sand. Its dusty streets are thronged by glum people. The market stalls are shabby, the stores run-down, old Daewoo taxis hoot ceaselessly (if you want to stand out in Peru's traffic, don't hoot!). The reek of rotting meat, of urine, of poverty and resignation pervades everything. We buy a few provisions and eat lunch in a restaurant directly on the square. My "suprema de pollo a Jerez" proves to be a chicken fillet slumped in a brown sauce that's as indefinable as it is unappetizing. Sabine's "ensalata mixta" is as lifeless as the desert outside the door.

Hours later we climb aboard a small single-engine propeller aircraft. Our pilot introduces himself as Gustavo and wears his sunglasses with that nonchalance that is unique to pilots. The aircraft taxis along a bumpy runway, takes off in a steep curve and simultaneously banks to the west. As we spot the first lines in the ground below us, I've already reached for the barf bag and have an unpleasant reunion with my "suprema de pollo a Jerez." I spend the whole of the half-hour flight either staring dazedly at a point just past the oil pressure dial or lowering my head to the bag, wretched and tormented, seeing nothing at all of the mysterious lines below us. In my brief lucid moments, I feel sorry for the pilot next to me. I spend the evening sunk in numb lethargy in the alcove of Lucy's cab. Sabine, who survived the flight astonishingly well, fixes herself some noodle soup. I have to look away as she eats. All the time the diesel engine next door throbs and roars unceasingly. It's time to leave the dismal Peruvian coast!

*Monotony between Lima and Nazca.*

*(unfortunately there are no photos of the lines at Nazca ...)*

127

# In the Highlands of Peru: Navel of the World

"In this world, we're all alike. But ...all like whom exactly?"
*Peruvian saying*

[km/miles 52,238/31,343 to 55,003/33,002]
Nasca – Tres Cruzes]

Opposite page: Indigenous inhabitants follow a religious procession in Cuzco. Top: Mystery in the streets of Arequipa.

After Camaná, around 300 kilometers (180 miles) south of Nazca, the Panamericana climbs to 2,300 meters (7,544 feet) – an ascent to brighter climes in more than the proverbial sense. We arrive in Arequipa, Peru's second largest city with a population of just under 90,000, and take a room in Hostal "La Casa de mi Abuela" ("my grandmother's house"). This pleasant, centrally located hotel has attractive rooms, large gardens, a pool and a fine restaurant in a beautiful little room with vaulted ceilings. We think we've earned it.

Arequipa is an absolutely enchanting old colonial town. It is dominated by the peak of El Misti, a perfectly conical volcano 5,821 meters (19,093 feet) high, and despite its size has a delightfully provincial air. We stroll through the pretty two-storey arcades which fringe three sides of Arequipa's main square and visit the immense cathedral of white sillar, a whitish volcanic stone, which towers above the fourth side of the square. The convent of Santa Catalina near the plaza transports us into a different era. As early as 1579, an entire district of the town of Arequipa was simply enclosed by a wall to create space and seclusion for 150 nuns and 400 maidservants. The events within these walls remained more or less hidden from the public for over four hundred years. Not until 1970 did the convent, by now reduced to seventeen nuns, reopen its doors. In those four hundred years of isolation its architecture had changed little, and

the entire complex was promptly designated a UNESCO World Heritage Site and lavishly renovated. Today we walk back in time into a bygone era. Perhaps the thick paint on the facades after renovation is a historical inaccuracy, but it looks lovely and even inspires me to dust off my replacement camera …!

To the east of Arequipa we climb the 4,800-meter (15,744 feet) pass of Patapampa before plunging into the breathtaking scenery of Cañon del Colca, which – depending on whether it's measured from the highest mountain peak near the gorge to Colca River or from the edge of the gorge – is 3,200 meters (10,496 feet) or 1,200 meters (3,936 feet) deep. We stand on the brink of a vast channel, watching powerful condors with wingspans of over 3 meters (10 feet) gliding over the abyss. The valley is composed of agricultural land where Indios till potato fields on skillfully terraced slopes, using the same simple wooden plows as their forefathers did. Here we are finally at the heart of Inca country, and now plan to tackle the seat of power of America's largest pre-Hispanic empire: Cuzco.

We arrive in the city, at an altitude of just under 3,400 meters (11,152 feet), in the late afternoon of a sunny day and establish a base camp for the next three weeks at a relatively comfortable campground – our first since Colombia – above the town center. At its zenith, the former capital of the Inca Empire

and "navel of the world" was at least as powerful, and probably richer, than Ancient Rome. Its magnificence must have been dazzling. An old chronicle describes the royal palaces as being covered with gold leaf. But 1533 saw the advent of the gold-hungry Spanish or, to be precise, Francisco Pizarro, heading an army that was inferior in numbers but superior in weaponry. The old story started all over again as the invaders conquered the empire, plundering and sacking the cities and building cathedrals and monasteries on their ruins in honor of a god whose teachings revolved around loving one's neighbor and avoiding violence.

On our first stroll through the old town on the afternoon of our arrival, we're permanently amazed. The cathedral on the gigantic Plaza de Armas is 85 meters (279 feet) long and 45 meters (148 feet) wide, and from the outside looks more like a fortress than a place of worship. However, it was built – and this is the truly amazing thing – on the foundation walls of the palace of the 8th Inca Viracocha. The huge ash-

lars were hewn so precisely that no mortar was needed; the blocks are stacked tightly without interstices and so skillfully dovetailed and bolted together that not even a sheet of paper would pass between them; and they bear cathedrals. Even by today's standards the architectural skills of the Incas which we encounter at every turn in Cuzco's old quarter are a baffling tour de force. We don't even know how the tons of stone blocks were transported; all that is known is that wheels were not used.

We spend almost a week in Cuzco visiting museums, churches and temples, eating in restaurants, washing clothes, browsing in book and CD stores, buying hand-woven fabrics from old market women, lazing around, taking photos; it's almost as if Peru had made its peace with us – or we with Peru. Traveling has become fun again. We buy tickets for the Backpacker Express on Saturday and board the train at six in the morning, alighting in Aquas Calientes after a four-hour journey and taking a room in a simple hotel. We stroll a little through the unspectacular town, walk along the Río Urubama in the afternoon, eat dinner on the plaza in the evening and go to bed early. Our alarm clock wakes us at five next morning, at five-thirty we are sitting sleepily in a bus… and twenty minutes later we're wide awake as we approach the most breathtaking, most baffling relic of the Incas: the ruined complex of Machu Picchu.

At an altitude of 2,470 meters (8,102 feet) amidst a world of steep, craggy mountains lies an Inca city as fascinating as it is mysterious. Three sides of the city are hemmed in by steep cliffs, lashed at their base by the wild waters of Río Urubama. Wayna Picchu looms at the north-western end like an enormous watchtower. Machu Picchu is in an ideal position to defend and control the entire valley – giving rise to the suspicion that there may have been something here to hide. But what? Experts are undecided. "Was the complex a summer resident of the Inca rulers, a refuge for the sun virgins, a city of wizards, an Inca university, a fortress defending against the wild tribes of the Amazon, or all of these at once?" wonders our guidebook. We pass the ticket barrier, climb a slight incline and reach a terrace from which we can survey South America's probably best-known and most dramatic photographic motif – and one which no photograph in the world can ever do justice to. Mist swirls up from the river, shrouding the ancient walls of the ruined city for minutes at a time before continuing to rise

Another 100 meters (328 feet) up to the pass!

*Above: Plaza de Armas in Cuzco with the cathedral (left) and La Compañia church.*

to the top of Wayna Picchu. The surrounding rocks plunge vertically into the depths. The first rays of sunshine penetrate the clouds for a few moments, highlighting points in the dark misty forests which clothe the mountains around Machu Picchu. We are in a place where nature and architecture have created an almost ethereal harmony, a perfect work of art of outstanding beauty.

Back in Cuzco, we fill our diesel tank and bid farewell to the ancient Inca city as we head east, descending after a two-hour drive into fertile Valle Sagrado de los Incas, the Incas' sacred valley. We drive along the valley through a downpour to the little town of Pisaq, finding a secure spot for the night in the garden of a hotel complex. Next morning a farmers' market is held on the village square; indigenous market women spread out their wares on the cobblestones and sell local valley produce – onions, maize, avocados, cabbage, herbs, potatoes, citrus

fruits, coca leaves and much more. It's a gloriously colorful, bustling spot. The people haggle passionately in Quechua, the language of the Incas, while seductive aromas spread through the square from the street food vendors. At the church we are present at a procession of the "alkaldes": the village elders and the mayor, wearing brightly colored traditional clothing, stand at the church door and graciously endure all of us travelers taking photos like crazy. By the time the tourist buses from Cuzco finally engulf the market square, we've already bought generous quantities of provisions and leave Pisaq in the early afternoon. A single-track dirt road leads up to 4,200 meters (13,776 feet), past steep fields where tilling is done with hand plows; past sparse fields where shepherd girls tend goats, alpaca and sheep; past small villages where people live in mud huts as they have done for centuries.

The villages gradually become more scattered, encounters with people rarer, the country-

Left: Salt terraces at Pichingote, the Incas' sacred valley.
Bottom left: Women spinning are a common sight in the Andean uplands.

side wilder. We are desperate to reach Tres Cruzes, a viewpoint at just under 4,000 meters (13,120 feet), before darkness falls, but heavy rain makes driving difficult on the muddy tracks and we make less than 20 kilometers'( 12 miles) progress in an hour. At some point we find ourselves in pitch darkness, and the rain is joined by fog which reduces visibility to a few meters.

Just as we're about to give up and spend the night at the roadside, we reach the road to Tres Cruzes. From here we have a further 13 kilometers (8 miles) to our parking spot for the night before, exhausted, we finally reach the viewpoint. We spot a little shelter at the end of the platform, candlelight visible inside. We've made it! Taking a deep breath, we drive to the shelter.

All ready for prosperous tourists ...

But the ground is too uneven to park here overnight. I reverse in the mud and succeed only in sinking Lucy up to the axles. Not even our four-wheel drive can help me out of this situation.

The people who now emerge from the shelter prove to be a group of five British tourists with a guide and driver. They watch as I vainly attempt to wrestle the vehicle out of the mud; some try to help by pushing from behind, but only get splashed in mud from head to toe from the spinning tires. Finally we hook Lucy up to a towrope and tie her to the group's tour bus, which stands a little higher on firm ground. The bus driver drives back and Lucy starts to heave herself out of the mud, meter by meter. We're almost there when the driver steers too far to the

Harmony of nature and architecture: the ancient Inca ruins at Machu Picchu

Tres Cruzes – well worth it ...

left and the bus leaves the road and threatens to plunge over the side itself, only restrained by Lucy's four-ton weight. Now it's Lucy that has to pull the bus out of its hair-raising position, which lands us back in the mud where we started. We try again; this time everything goes fine and finally both vehicles are back on secure ground.

This emergency assistance is deemed worthy of breaking out our last half-bottle of premium tequila from Mexico. We share the exquisite liquor with the group in the shelter, drinking out of tin cups. It warms us, relaxes us and feels good – very good. We soon retire to Lucy, heat the previous day's leftover potato and vegetable stew and go to bed. At almost 4,000 meters (13,120 feet), the night is bitterly cold and the thin air makes for restless sleep. Our alarm clock rings at five. Sabine stays in bed while I peel off the cozy warm blanket, throw on a few clothes and go

outside into the icy dawn. Walking up a hill with my camera, I find myself surveying a different world.

Before me, the Andes plunge over 3500 meters (11,480 feet) into the lowlands of the Amazon basin. Above is an almost unbroken carpet of cloud, below me the steaming jungle of the world's largest rainforest. Between the two is the clear morning air which seems to glow for a few seconds, ignited by the rising sun before it disappears again behind a wall of gray cloud. Another picture that's impossible to capture on film. But this moment, this brief time is the reason why we so urgently wanted to spend the night up here.

And it was worth all the effort! I stand there taking pictures (I can't help it) and sink into a confused reverie over travel, the lust for adventure, the price we occasionally pay and the lifelong rewards which we carry within us. Far below me a green universe extends, the world's Garden of Eden. That's where we're going today. This is where the adventure begins!

0 ——— 30 miles
0 ——— 50 km

PERU

Manu NP
Pilcopata
Rio Alto
Madre de Dios
Tres Cruzes
Amazonia

# Amazonia: The Sultry Universe

*"If we could only comprehend a single flower, we would know who we are and what this world is."*
Jorge Luis Borges, Argentine writer

[km/miles 55,003/33,002 to 55,211/33,127|
Tres Cruzes – Amazonia – Tres Cruzes]

*As reliable as any alarm clock: at Villa Carmen hacienda the screech of the blue and gold macaw wakes us every morning.*

After spending a freezing night at an altitude of almost 4,000 meters (13,120 feet), at sunrise the next morning the ladies are slow to get going. Sabine conceals her distaste at such an early start behind a cloak of silence as we pack up, but Lucy is less tactful: her 6,900 cc need air, and that's precisely what is in short supply up here. In protest, she splutters and pants and knocks, and fills Tres Cruzes full of exhaust fumes as if she were trying to outdo the banks of swirling mist rising from the valley. Steep as the sides of a cauldron, the slopes of the mountain crest plunge down to the plain 3,500 meters (11,480 feet) below. We are standing on the western border of Amazonia, at the gateway to Manu National Park, almost four million acres in size and thus half the size of Switzerland, with the most richly varied array of flora and fauna of any rainforest reserve in the world.

We slowly coast along. A muddy single-track path clings to the brown flank of an Andean peak before gradually dipping into the abyss. After climbing a few meters in altitude we enter a landscape that couldn't be more different from the barren tundra of Peru's highlands. Mountainous cloud forests spread over the mountain peaks, where dark clouds become entangled in the canopy of tree crowns before struggling free to rise once more. At the side of our washed-out track, ravines plummet into a bottomless abyss, lush and overgrown. Occa-sionally we see the flash of a stream along their floors, rushing from the icy upper slopes to the great rivers of the plains, Río Manu and Madre de Dios; the region has water in abundance, trickling, raging and flowing to merge sooner or later with the mother of all rivers, the Amazon. This mighty watercourse is fed by over 1,000 tributaries, forming the most extensive network of waterways in the world. At the coast around 6,000 kilometers (3,600 miles) east of the track down which we are currently jolting, it pours around 180,000 cubic meters (6,354000 cubic feet) of water into the Atlantic every second – more than all the next largest rivers in the world (Congo, Niger, Zambezi, Yangtze, Brahmaputra and Orinoco) combined – and yet this immense volume accounts for a mere quarter of all the water in the Amazonian river system. The rest evaporates, is sucked up into thirsty tree trunks or exuded by foliage, condenses to form cloud, is precipitated as rain and thus keeps the whole dynamic cycle in motion.

It's always raining somewhere or other in Amazonia. Today it just happens to be exactly where we're churning through the mud, slowing our progress as Lucy skids from one slippery pothole to the next. Every 300 meters (984 feet) the temperature rises by around two degrees Celsius. Gigantic walls of entwined trees jut into the sky along the track, laden from top to bottom with mosses, ferns and orchids. Manu

National Park boasts 200 different species of tree per hectare – the whole of Europe has only 160. We descend step by step. Lucy's windshield is like a screen showing a breathtaking film. We take short breaks again and again to "stop the film" for a few minutes; only when the diesel en-

gine falls silent do the voices of the forest become audible – birds whistling and cawing, water splashing and gurgling, wind rustling the foliage and making the tree trunks creak. We breathe in the scents of the forest, sometimes moldy and sweet, at other times astringent and spicy. Occasionally we could have sworn we could smell herbs. Wasn't that a whiff of rosemary? A trace of thyme?

Eventually the sun triumphs over the mist and the valley broadens out. We reach Madre de Dios River, gray-blue and torrential and, in memory of its source 2,000 meters (6,560 feet) above, ice-cold. Soon, when it has left the Andes behind, it will grow more serene and course sluggishly eastward. At Manaus in Brazil, 1,000 kilometers (600 miles) to our east, its waters will mingle with the Amazon before embarking on a

*Above: Down, down all the way for every 300-meter (984 feet) drop in altitude the temperature rises by one degree Celsius.*
*Left: It's always raining somewhere in Amazonia.*

further journey of 4,000 kilometers (2400 miles) to the Atlantic, descending at the rate of a few centimeters (inches) per kilometer (mile). Manaus, far from the coast, is only 26 meters (85 feet) above sea level.

In the early afternoon we reach Pilcopata, a forest village straight out of a storybook with its dusty roads, rambling stray dogs, huts lashed together from lumber with tarpaulin canopies as protection from the rain or the burning sun, under which dark-skinned men doze away the slow, hot midday, shirts open to the waist. We feel their eyes upon us as we drive down the main street. A wooden hut has a veranda before it on which a table and two chairs stand, the sign over it proclaiming "Restaurant". As we sit down we're welcomed by lean, rangy Raoul offering grilled fish or grilled chicken, and we decide on fish and order a cold "cerveza" to wash it down. We're rooted to the spot for hours, unable

to tear ourselves away from the veranda as we observe the sleepy activity all around us. Raoul tells us that today, Monday, is a quiet day, but on Tuesdays and Fridays a truck of goods comes from Cuzco; a market takes place and the village gets pretty busy.

We decide to stay in Pilcopata for a few days. Our guidebook recommends the accommodation at "Villa Carmen," an old hacienda a little way outside the village where simple "cabañas" can be rented; perhaps we can park Lucy there. But we can't find the way. After several trips around the village we ask a young taxi-driver called Elvis, who tells us, "Go down through the river, and on the other side you'll see the road to the hacienda." We follow his advice and arrive at a big old wooden house with a red corrugated iron roof and a shady veranda, set in a lush, blooming garden with a lake shaded by a spreading willow, all amid the dense rain-

Left: Shopping in Pil-
copata. The general
store has lukewarm
Coke.
Bottom left: At the
gas station, we buy
diesel in old paint
buckets.

forest. Gretel, the sixty-year-old owner, comes out to meet and welcome us, showing us a spot where we can camp and inviting us to dinner on her veranda to meet her husband Abel. Some hours later, we're sitting in the humid evening air under the scant light of a fluorescent tube battered by eager moths and mosquitoes. Gretel serves fish from their own lake baked in banana leaves and rice with vegetables cooked in bamboo stems. She is an outstanding cook, and Abel is a hospitable and tireless storyteller – although he mutters more than he talks and growls as though his vocal chords were in a knot. This doesn't exactly make the conversation in Spanish any easier, but we understand that the two of them have lived on this hacienda for forty years; their children have long left the nest. They work an area of 7,500 acres di-

Three monkeys fighting over a hammock

rectly bordering the National Park, living from their pineapple, coffee, banana and chestnut plantations and from occasional tourism. The couple employs twenty staff, the majority lowland Indians from the Piro tribe who have built huts on Abel's land.

We spend four unforgettable days at "Hazienda Villa Carmen," accompanying Abel on expeditions through the country with his foreman Ephraim, a modest, amiable indigena with a grin as broad as the Amazon itself. We march through the forest, Ephraim ahead of us

141

hacking a narrow path through the dense jungle with his machete. Abel tells us tales of Amazonia, its natural life and its people. Both men demonstrate the technique of drawing bucketfuls of fish from the surrounding waters – including piranhas, which are only half as dangerous as their reputation but twice as tasty. We go horseback riding at sunset through the pineapple groves, gallop across meadows and follow narrow trails through the forest, and Gretel serves us delicious Amazon home cooking.

Time flies, and we could stay here for weeks, but we have to leave. Our Peruvian visas are only valid for another seven days and we have a long way to go before the Bolivian border. We take our leave of Gretel and Abel and Ephraim and the other staff, exchanging addresses and promising each other that we'll stay in touch. When we finally depart and leave the country on the same narrow track on which we had ridden like gauchos (well, that's what it felt like to us…) the previous day, we feel no pleasure at moving on. We fill up our diesel tank in the village (from a bucket with a tube and a scrap of fabric as a filter) and finally embark on the long journey back to the highlands, from an altitude of under 500 meters (1,640 feet) to over 4,000 (13,120 feet). Lucy tackles the ascent as if it were nothing more than a stroll in the park.

Once again we spend the night in the freezing heights of Tres Cruzes where our expedition into the Amazon basin had begun a few days earlier. Once again we sleep fitfully in the thin air, and the next morning none of us can really get going.

Sabine sits in silence, Lucy fills the Andes with exhaust fumes - and me? I stare into the valley and dream of the life of a gaucho!

# Bolivia: Lucy in Heaven

"May what your eyes see never leave your heart!"
*Saying of the Aimara people*

[km/miles 55,211/333,127 to 59,220/35,532|
Tres Cruzes – Uyuni]

*Young woman on island of Taquile in Lake Titicaca.*

But now we have to get going! Our Peruvian visas expire in a few days. It's time to leave this country.

We cross the treeless upland basin of the "altiplano" and reach Lake Titicaca, shared by Bolivia and Peru and believed to be the highest navigable lake in the world. Lying at an altitude of 3,800 meters (12,464 feet) in this colorless land, the flawless sapphire of its waters vies with the blue sky stretching over the Andes. We make time for just one more stop on the Peruvian side of the border; in the unassuming town of Puno, we board a little motorboat and sail out into the lake past the floating reed islands of the Uro people. These islands, composed of reed bundles lashed together, were used by the Uro during the Inca era as a refuge from the mighty northern invaders. Subsisting on the fish and birds they caught, the Uro developed an autonomous lifestyle on their artificial islands, and their descendants still live there today.

Further out, in the middle of the lake, we visit Taquile. For the 1,400 or so indigenous inhabitants of the islands, everyday life is bound by ancient customs and strict rules. The "Taquileños" still practice terrace agriculture today and sell their local produce, primarily potatoes and the local root vegetable "oca," at the market in Puno. But the island's main claim to fame is its knitting men, who can be seen leaning their backs against the mud walls in the vil-

lage square, silently absorbed in their craft. They produce beautiful pullovers and caps, knitted with immense skill and artistry.

We drive along Lake Titicaca towards the south-east, heading for the Bolivian border. The formalities on both sides go smoothly. The Bolivian police officer who notes my driver's license details after we cross the border promptly asks me for a donation to the Widows' and Orphans' Fund – or the Virgin Mary or the local women's soccer team, it could be anything, really – it's a standard South American ritual.

The pretty border town of Copacabana is the home of a strange rite performed every morning in front of the cathedral. The inhabitants park their cars on the street and decorate them with plastic flowers and garlands. A priest carrying a tin bucket of holy water then emerges from the cathedral and blesses the vehicles. Of course we and Lucy have to join the line, edging in between minibuses and taxis; we dress Lucy up like a carnival float for her blessing by the white-clad priest. To complete the ritual, we open a bottle of beer and spray it over Lucy's hood (drinking the last drops ourselves, in line with the local custom!). A small donation is pressed into the priest's hand and we leave Lake Titicaca with a blissful smile on our lips.

We head west across the "altiplano" along a dead straight road, which soon expands into an eight-lane "avenida" passing through sprawling

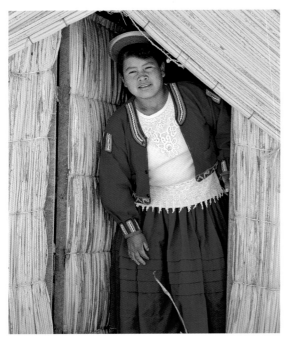

suburbs of rough, unrendered brick buildings. Suddenly, at an altitude of 4,000 meters (13,120 feet), the road stops abruptly at the edge of a vast basin and plunges 600 meters (1,968 feet) into its depths: La Paz.

Bolivia's largest metropolis is the seat of its national government (but not the capital city: that's Sucre) and is probably the strangest city complex in the world. Skyscrapers jut up from the base of the enormous natural basin, its sides densely crowded with buildings right to the top. Not an attractive city, but an exciting one. We take a small hotel room near the center and spend three days exploring the city – and we're in luck: this weekend La Paz celebrates its 458th anniversary with a gorgeous procession. Carnival folklore groups known as "Morenadas" progress down the Avenida Mariscal Santa Cruz to the throbbing rhythm of brass bands. Female dancers wear bowler hats and precious little else,

*Above and left: The descendants of the Uru people still live on floating "islands" made from hand-roped bundles of reeds.*

*Above: Lucy is twice blessed in Copacabana – once by the Catholic priest (left) and once by a local shaman (right).*
*Right: The ferry taking us around the south-east tip of Lake Titicaca inspires little confidence.*

while their male counterparts conceal their faces behind fierce masks and sweat under the thirty or so kilograms of their brightly embroidered fantasy costumes. It's a colorful and noisy spectacle, and we sway along and fall under its spell. In the meantime, Lucy is in the garage of Ernesto Hug, a Bolivian of Swiss extraction who runs what must be the cleanest workshop by far in the whole of Latin America. She gets another full-scale service – and she'll need it when we leave La Paz.

We plan to take the "most dangerous road in the world" (according to a study by the Inter-American Development Bank) to the Yungas, the hot, tropical Andean valley region. From there our route runs through isolated wilderness into the Bolivian lowlands. A long, often lonely, difficult stretch lies ahead of us. We fill all our fuel and water tanks to the brim, stock up with plenty of provisions, take a deep breath and… set off. The journey is harmless to start with, initially taking us up to the snowy pass of La Cumbre at an altitude of 4,700 meters (15,416 feet).

However, from here we head down again, leaving the barren crags behind and immersing ourselves in a world of bromeliads and tree ferns. Soon the asphalt comes to an end and the serpentines grow tighter until the road becomes a single track. From now on we must drive on the left when there is oncoming traffic; to our right is the steep, soaring rock face, but to our left, on the brink of an almost sheer drop of 800 meters (2,624 feet) into the depths, are the passing places – and whoever is driving downhill has to

let the other driver pass. Not for the faint-hearted! At the edge of the road small metal crucifixes with nameplates, some decorated with fresh flowers, stand in memory of many a last journey. Over a hundred people die along this stretch every year.

In three days of driving, we traverse a 4,000-meter (13,120 feet) difference in altitude along bumpy tracks, through practically the whole palette of South America's climate and vegetation zones from snow to steamy rainforest, be-

fore reaching the lowlands of Beni. Down here we pass through a region of humid savanna, hot, sticky and prone to flooding during the rainy season. Although now level, the track is no easier to negotiate; the short but heavy showers transform it into a greasy, slippery slide. We skid through the mud at walking pace and try to avoid drifting into the swamp – and that's when we encounter another problem, as swarms of aggressive mosquitoes invade our slowly progressing driver's cab. They are so bad that we're forced to close the windows and feel as if we're trapped in a sauna. But the rich wildness of the landscape all around us is breathtaking: storks, jaribus, cormorants, ibis, spoonbills, moorhens and parrots dwell in the swamp, lakes and forest which border the track. The water is said to be home to caymans and anacondas eight to 9 meters (29.5 feet) long, warns our guidebook. The friendly, cheerful inhabitants are largely "Macheteros," descendants of the lowland Indians, who speak their own language and live in modest, palm-thatched huts. The men incessantly

*Above: The different styles in which the Taquileños wear their hand-knitted caps are said to indicate their marital status.*
*Left: Literally running out of air while hiking across Isla del Sol at an altitude of 4,000 meters (13,120 feet).*

"Happy Birthday, La Paz!"

chew coca leaves, their habit betrayed by their bulging cheeks, dark-stained lips and terrible teeth. We cross the broad Río Mamoré on a wooden raft pushed by a canoe fitted with an outboard motor. Once again we struggle through deep craters and muddy potholes before reaching the little town of Trinidad after four days' driving and finding ourselves on a tarred road again. Ahhh, that's good! You have to have spent days on wretched roads to understand just how precious a decent tarred road is!

To the south of Santa Cruz – once an outpost of civilization, today Bolivia's boom town – the smiles are wiped off our faces again. A stony track leads up into the Andes, back into the Bolivian highlands. Today is Saturday. We have to get some mileage behind us because we don't want to miss the Sunday market in the mountain village of Tarabuco, so that we have many hours' driving ahead. Lucy's radiator is leaking. Not too badly, but a harmless crack can soon develop into an unpleasant problem on these rough trails. In ad-

dition, the front axle is making a disquieting rattling noise. We drive until after dark and spend the night at the side of the road in lofty solitude. As soon as the sun rises the next morning we pack up, top up the radiator (fortunately the crack hasn't widened) and clatter at top speed down the road to Tarabuco. We park Lucy at the edge of the village and work our way on foot through the bustling activity to the market place. The lanes of the village are thronged with market stalls jostling each other for space. "Campesinos" from the entire region are vociferously buying and selling fruit, vegetables, meat, fabrics, leather goods, tools, jewelry, building materials … everything necessary for life in the mountains. The Indios are clad in glowing colors, the men wearing hand-woven ponchos, helmet-like headgear, silver-buckled leather belts and spurred wooden shoes while the women, swathed in dark cloaks, boast angular hats embroidered with fine spangles and featuring beaded "curtains" at the sides which conceal half the wearer's face. The people here are proud, reacting dismissively or even aggressively to my request for permission to take photos – or demanding a reasonable fee. But they're right! The few coins won't hurt us.

*Above: Down the "most dangerous road in the world" to the Yungas, Bolivia's hot, tropical Andean valleys.*
*Right: Campesinos selling coca leaves at Tarabuco market.*

We let ourselves be carried along by the bustling crowds until early afternoon, then return exhausted to Lucy and embark on the last ninety minutes of our journey to the old colonial city of Sucre. Once there, we rent a room in a pretty hotel in the old quarter and treat ourselves to a few days' well-earned rest. After our wild ride over the last few days, Sucre is the perfect place to relax. Whitewashed colonial houses line cobbled streets leading past churches and little squares, all ending at Plaza 25 de Mayo: it's reminiscent of Old Spain. We stroll through the shady Parque Boliviar and spend some tranquil moments in the Iglesia La Merced before the magnificent Renaissance-style Altar of St John before climbing the bell tower to absorb the magnificent view over the Ciudad Blanca. We drink an ice-cold Erdinger wheat beer in "Joyride" café and track down "El Germén," a little restaurant in Calle San Alberto, where we feast on German vegetarian food – and can patriotically confirm that after "trucha" and "anticuchos, cuy" and "cebiche," "choclos, salteñas, huatia" and beans in every variation known to

a population of around 160,000 in the year 1650 – greater than Madrid, Paris or Rome at the time. Yet the city's wealth was stained with blood. Around eight million forced laborers, primarily indigenas but also slaves from Africa, had died in the mines by the 18th century. Potosí's might soon crumbled as the supply of silver from the mountain faltered and failed, and its population fell to below 10,000. Today thirty-six partly ruined churches alone bear witness to the former extent of the city's wealth. The city's historic center was designated a World Heritage Site by UNESCO. Although tin and silver ore is still dug out of Cerro Rico de Potosí, now honeycombed through and through, no-one gets rich from it any more. I take a guided tour to one of the mines. Sabine saves herself the effort – and is proved right. Our group of ten, all clad in protective clothing and safety helmets, toils through narrow gangways until we are deep within the mountain. In some areas the chutes are so narrow that we have to slide down on our backs. Temperatures rise meter by meter until they exceed thirty degrees, and the dust and

man, a fresh spinach and tofu stir-fry from our home country tastes positively ambrosial.

After four days – Lucy's radiator is now patched up, the rattling from the front axle partially fixed – we move 160 kilometers (96 miles) further on to Potosí, the highest metropolis in the world at an altitude of 4,065 meters (13,333 feet). Potosí owes its existence to a mountain; the mines of Cerro Rico de Potosí, 4,829 meters (15,839) high, yielded 46,000 tons of silver from the mid-16th century onward. With a reputation as America's treasure-chamber, Potosí had

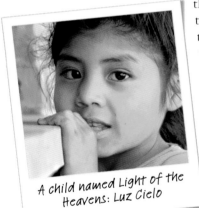

*Right: Smile of relief – after a strenuous visit to the silver mines at Potosí. Below right: Miners at Cerro Rico. Opposite page: "La Ciudad Blanca" – Sucre.*

*A child named Light of the Heavens: Luz Cielo*

thin air make progress laborious, a genuine torture. Hundreds of "mineros" still work in the mountain under these wretched conditions. They boost their energy reserves by ceaselessly chewing coca leaves, pushing their wracked bodies to the limits of physical endurance and beyond. A miner is considered unfit for work after an average of fifteen years in these mines. We spend two hours in this hell, battling claustrophobia, shortness of breath and sweating attacks, and experience blissful relief when the mountain spits us out again.

"Sumaq Orqo" is its name in Quechua, "beautiful mountain." A name it doesn't deserve any more!

Only a little over half a day's drive separates the murky depths of Cerro Rico de Potosí from the dazzling glare of Salar de Uyuni. The largest salt pans in the world stretch over south-west Bolivia like an enormous pure white starched sheet. They are the dried-up remains of the enormous inland salt lake of the Andes, Lago Minchins. A crust of salt 160 kilometers (96 miles) long, 135 kilometers (81 miles) wide and up to 7 (22 feet) meters thick covers the "altiplano." We roar over a completely level, empty plain at 80 kilometers (48 miles) per hour, with nothing to restrict our view. The only boundary is the knife-edge of the horizon where the petrified earth meets an infinite steel-blue sky. We actually believe we can see the earth's curve. There are no birds, no reptiles, not even a solitary insect: only the powerful gusts of the chill wind all around us. We spend the night amid this "white sea," as the locals call the Salar, the boundless, twinkling stars of the night sky arching above us. The wind gradually drops, and we are surrounded by an unearthly calm, a silence like none we have never heard before. No rustling, no rushing, no chirping, no humming – nothing. Perfect silence. In an infinite empty space. Peace!

Crossing the lake at eighty km/h: Salar de Uyuni

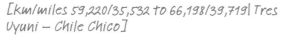

# Chile – An Island in the Continent

"Anyone who hasn't been in the Chilean forest doesn't know this planet."

Pablo Neruda, Chilean author

[km/miles 59,220/35,532 to 66,198/39,719| Tres Uyuni – Chile Chico]

All the insignia required of a true Chilean caballero – hat, poncho, mustache.

South of Uyuni, the track we planned to take to the Chilean border plays a dirty trick on us by gradually sinking into the salty brown earth and eventually disappearing altogether. We stop in the middle of the arid desert and get out. A barren plain extends in all directions, with no sign of a road far and wide. I take out my binoculars and look around: in the distance to the south is a herd of vicuñas, foraging for fodder in this wasteland, and behind them I can make out a black line. It must be the railroad, a relic of the past when trains ran between Antofagasta/Chile and Bolivia. Amazingly, even today an occasional train rumbles from Calama in Chile to Uyuni. We need to use the railroad tracks as orientation; if we follow them, we can't miss the isolated border outpost.

We make straight for the line across the plain and turn to the south-west along the tracks, gradually climbing to higher altitudes and eventually spotting a few buildings along the tracks and a toll bar behind them. Not exactly a hub of activity. Parts of old trains and rusting rails are scattered in the dust, the windowpanes are broken and the wind whistles between old brick walls. A solitary, diminutive Bolivian border guard holds the fort in a shabby office. We shake hands in greeting, chat a little and hand him a bag of fruit, vegetables and coca leaves – none of which we are permitted to

take into Chile. The emigration formalities are quickly completed, and we shake hands again and leave Bolivia behind us.

After a few hundred meters through no man's land, we emerge into another planet, as Chile welcomes us with a broad, smooth tarred road, lined with trimly plastered border offices where staff sit in front of computers. Formalities are dealt with efficiently and punctiliously; no fees are charged, no donations requested. After half an hour we are heading down a flawless Chilean road towards Calama. And when we do find potholes, a sign posted several meters ahead gives us advance warning. When was the last time we experienced that? On the A27 going to Bremerhaven – if at all!

In Calama, an unattractive mining town 200 kilometers (120 miles) from the border, culture shock catches up. No more children yelling "Gringo" at us, a cry that has accompanied us constantly since Mexico; here the men lift their hand in what is uncomfortable reminiscent of a Hitler salute! In the shopping mall glittering with Christmas decorations, German Christmas carols warble in cheesy Latino muzak versions, and the Asian snack bar on the second floor of the food court stocks Paulaner beer. We briefly consider returning to Bolivia!

Chile is considered the richest country in the continent, and its inhabitants are often

dubbed the Prussians of South America. Its proportions are jaw-dropping: Chile measures a sensational 4,300 kilometers (2,580 miles) in length from north to south – farther than from Hammerfest to Palermo – yet is an average of only 180 kilometers (108 miles) wide. Chileans like to describe their country as an island, cut off by the Pacific in the west and the Atacama Desert (alleged to be the driest in the world) in the north; the snowy crags of the Andes rise into the sky in the east, and at the southern tip of Chile the end of the world begins.

We roar along (or the equivalent of roaring along, given Lucy's sluggishness) to reach Santiago de Chile as fast as possible. Our haste stems from the fact that Sabine suddenly needs to fly to the USA on family matters. One-third of all Chileans live in the country's capital, a total of six million people. When we pass the city borders after a few days, one city dweller – a bus driver – manages to make us hate him immediately. He rams into us at a junction in his old jalopy, brakes sharply, checks his rear view mirror, shrugs his shoulders and roars off. What the heck is wrong with Latin American bus drivers?

*Above: Still-life – llama at Lascan volcano.*
*Left: Men amongst themselves at San Pedro de Atacama.*

*Above: We head south on the Argentinian side, passing Valle de la Luna.*
*Right: Good place for an emergency stop – street life in easy-going Santiago de Chile.*
*Opposite page top: In the wine country Chile, a heavenly Sauvignon Blanc grows in a majestic setting.*

Does their job profile specify "inconsiderate jackass," or do they have some genetic defect? Poor old Lucy has taken it bravely, but her front offside wing is in bad shape; one auxiliary lamp is lying on the road, the bumper is pretty twisted and the fender is badly dented. I drop Sabine at the airport and Lucy at the garage, and find myself a hotel room. Our enforced break lasts a week, giving me time to digest the excitement of the past few weeks and creating the mental space I need to welcome new adventures.

As soon as Sabine returns we waste no time in heading south, gliding along the smoothly asphalted Panamericana. The four-lane expressway is Chile's main arterial road, running the length of the country. And it's as safe as a Bavarian convent: no guerrillas lying in wait to kidnap tourists, no drug rings defending their territory, no corrupt police demanding donations – instead, emergency telephones every few kilometers. Hardly a real adventure at all! To the south of the town of Los Angeles begins Chile's "little south," a wonderland of lakes,

mountains and dense forests. The days grow longer and the temperatures fall with every kilometer south that we travel. We change down a gear and coast easily through this idyllic landscape, where the chief settlers were 19th-century German emigrants as the architecture clearly shows. Instead of the flat roofs and patios that

generally feature in Spanish colonial buildings, we find gables and slate roofs. And we feel closer to home in other ways, too; the inhabitants occasionally address us in German, the supermarkets stock Haribo gummy bears, and "Hotel Seehaus" in Frutillar serves "Torta de Selva Negra," Black Forest gateau, daily. We drive no more than a few hours per day and soon scope out a place to camp, setting up at crystalline lakes with names like Lago Rapel, Lago Llanquihue or Lago Todos Los Santos. We usually have a view of snow-capped mountains and volcanoes towering like guards on the opposite banks, and stroll a little along lava-blackened shores or huddled beech woods. Or we hire kayaks and paddle through inky blue waters. Or sit in our camping chairs reading and savoring a glass of excellent Chilean Chardonnay with a few olives, a little cheese and wholegrain bread from the German baker in the next town.

A ferry departing from the village of Pargua deposits us on Isla Grande de Chiloé. The island is 180 kilometers (108 miles) long – and it's 180 kilometers (108 miles) of pure rain. The stormy Pacific gales that incessantly chase gray banks of clouds over the island have shaped the islanders, so familiar to us from our years in Tasmania: slightly rough, slightly eccentric, slightly oddly dressed, hesitant to show friendship but after a while hearty and warm. We love the island from the moment we set foot on it. A little way south of its capital of Castro, we rent a cozy "cabaña" raised on thin stilts directly at the water's edge.

In the late afternoon when the tide goes out, we sit on our balcony and watch dolphins hunting in the shallow water. Just before darkness falls, the sun actually breaks through the clouds and bathes the countryside in a liquid golden light. From now on the sun is an increasingly frequent companion. We dust off the scooter and explore the whole island, passing brightly painted slate-roofed houses, bays where tiny fishing boats run aground at low tide, and

*The stuff that dream(wine)s are made on ...*

beautiful old wooden churches, some built by the Jesuits as early as the 17th century. On the weekend we visit a rodeo outside the little village of Chonchi. In a small arena seating no more than a few hundred, we cram ourselves onto plain wooden benches between fishermen and farmers and watch the "caballeros" battle it out. Unlike North American rodeos, the aim here is not to ride wild horses or bulls, but to demonstrate skill and the art of dressage. Two riders must try to drive an enraged bull to a particular point in the arena using only their horses, without whips or lassos. While one urges the bull forward, the other must gradually drive it over to the required spot, riding at an angle to the bull – and all this at a gallop. It's mainly a test of deportment and control.

The experience is a magnificently self-absorbed, harmonious village fiesta. Families unpack picnics on their benches, teenagers perched on wooden fences pay more attention to the opposite sex than to the show, children tumble around between the stalls selling hats, boots and spurs that could be part of medieval armor. Melancholy Latino music blares tinnily from loudspeakers, and the atmosphere in the arena is no more excited than at a meeting of the town libraries committee. Chileans have little of the flamboyant enthusiasm of other Latin American peoples. They are regarded as reserved – with a more "northern" temperament.

In the little town of Quellón in the island's south, we drive Lucy onto another ferry, this time taking us across the Gulf of Ancud to Chaitén. There we start our journey along the Carretera Austral, a lonely track twisting for 1,200 kilometers (720 miles) through wild, primeval country, past deep blue lakes and icy glaciers, dark forests, jagged fjords and snow-capped volcanoes.

Left and bottom left: German Chile in the open-air museum of "Colonia Aleman" in Frutillar.

After four generations in Chile, his native language is German!

Chaitén proves to be a plain little one-horse town with single-storey wooden houses, its oversized "avenidas" indicating that the town planners originally had other intentions. And yet it's located in a glorious spot, between the sea and the mountains. The volcano of Michimáhuida towers to the north-east, Corcovado to the south – it's easy to guess what the planners had in mind. 4 kilometers (2,5 miles) to the north of Chaitén our guidebook recommends a campground with power hook-up and hot showers directly on the beach. We set up camp on a grassy meadow a few meters from a pebbly shore, just in time for the sunset. The sun's pale disc sinks over the sea, bathing the land in soft magenta and adding a glow of silver to the foaming whitecap waves. In the distance Corcovado rises almost symmetrical from the water, while close at hand, before our very eyes, dolphins leap out of the water and play in the surf. We watch them and a nearby sea-lion colony through our binoculars – and all this while we're at the dinner table… Chile's wild south has welcomed us with a magnificent overture!

The next morning we aim for Carretera Austral. The first few kilometers south of Chaitén are asphalted, but soon the road narrows and Lucy finds herself bumping down a single-track dirt road, following the Río Yelcho first through green pastures, then through dark forests. The sky is cloudy and a cold wind whistles through the valley; traffic is rare, and the countryside is wild and deserted. We set up camp at the edge of Lago Yelcho, a somber glacial lake, don raincoats and heavy shoes and hike along its pebbly shore until dense virgin

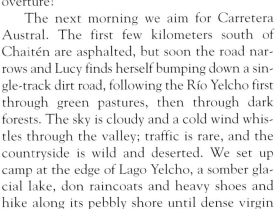

Right and bottom right: Points are deducted if the hat falls off – the rodeo at Chonchi on the island of Chiloé is a self-absorbed, harmonious village festival.

Keeping the kids out of danger.

forest extending to the water's edge makes further progress impossible. Back at camp we light a fire and grill half a salmon, bought in Quellón at the fish market. The fresh breeze blows the acrid smoke into my eyes – but I have a brainwave and put on my diving goggles, this evening using them for a rather different purpose than their intended one.

We cross Queulat National Park, turn into a narrow side track and camp near Ventisquero Colgante, the "Hanging Glacier." Next morning we pack some provisions into a rucksack and climb up to the glacier. Our path initially takes us across a shaky suspension bridge then ascends steeply upward through cold South Chilean rain forest through a murky world of lichens and ferns, beech forest, groves of fuchsia and bamboo and the mighty pangue plant, similar to our rhubarb. The stems are cooked and eaten like rhubarb, but the enormous leaves are as big as cabin roofs. After almost two hours the trail ends abruptly at a cliff edge. Almost simultaneously, the sun struggles to break through the clouds. Some way ahead, the tongue of the

Colgante glacier extends over the crest between two mountains. A blue-white waterfall thunders into the depths from the icy masses, pouring into a milky lake several hundred meters below. It's such a perfect scene that it would be the ideal backdrop for a dinosaur skeleton in a natural history museum.

Around the sleepy provincial capital of Coyhaique, the Carretera Austral is asphalted and Lucy can take a breather. We cruise through rolling pastures which were still impenetrable virgin forest at the end of the 19th century. In

1937 the Chilean government passed a law concerning colonization of the province which stated that land may only pass into private ownership when it is fully cleared. The few settlers lost no time, slashing and burning large areas of the forest within only a few years. Even today charred stumps jut like monuments from the hills amid grazing Holstein cattle. We bounce over a corrugated iron track which, although dusty, is easy to negotiate in all but a few areas. The road winds along Valle del Río Simpson through swampy lagoons and moorland, rises to an altitude of 1,100 meters (3,608 feet) and is accompanied for a while by the bizarre panorama of Cerro Castillo, a clutter of rocky crags up to 2,675 meters (8,774 feet) high and perched amid the rampant forest like a crazy fortress. We finally reach the shores of Lago General Carrera, its waters shimmering turquoise in the rays of the late afternoon sun.

To its west, the steep peaks of the southern Andes rise up to over 4,000 meters (13,120 feet), while its east – on Argentine soil – extends into the level desert steppes of Patagonia. During the night we spend here on the lakeshore, we gain our first experience of the infamous Patagonian winds, which howl around our camp, make Lucy shake like a goose's butt and whip the waters of Lago General Carrera into ocean-sized waves.

A parting lies ahead of us: we are leaving the Andes behind, these magnificent mountains which have accompanied us for months since Colombia. While we will still come close to their outlying foothills, at the Fitzroy Massif or Torres del Paine National Park further to the south, we will no longer climb their passes, breathe their thin air, or see the stars in such proximity – a realization that makes us thoughtful and a little melancholy. Our memories of

*Colorful wooden houses at Castro, the little island capital of Chiloé, are reminiscent of Scandinavia.*

*Right: In Chile's wet south, the giant leaves of the pangue make perfect umbrellas.*
*Bottom right: Ferry from Quellón to Chaitén.*
*Opposite page top: Spectacular overnight camp at Chiloé.*
*Bottom: At Lago General Carrera we gradually bid the Andes farewell.*

South America will be inseparably entwined with our memories of the world of the Andes.

We drive around the southern end of Lago General Carrera and take a spectacular shore road toward the Argentine border, arriving in the afternoon at the plain town of Chile-Chico directly on the lakeshore. This backwater basically consists of yet another completely oversized main street. In its center section, where the supermarket, Internet café and bus stop are gathered, shabby loudspeakers are suspended from which noisy music pours day and night. The passion that all Latin Americans have for cheesy music played over wretched sound systems occasionally takes on pathological dimensions. Music is everywhere at all times of day and night, always played over tinny, clattering loudspeakers. In his book "The Old Patagonian Express," Paul Theroux posits the bold theory that Latinos continuously listen to music to avoid the need to think. While we don't take things that far, it is true that thinking is not made any easier against the continual din. So we sit in the Internet café in Chile-Chico with the racket of the loudspeakers outside and a radio blaring away inside and I find myself unable to write a single line.

We spend the night in the orchard of a "hostal," far enough away from the town center and its music. Here, at the edge of the Patagonian desert, it is bitterly cold.

We soon retreat into our cabin, cook up a simple potato fry, open a bottle of red wine with our dinner and afterwards swathe ourselves in blankets, light a candle and open our books. Sabine has brought the new John Irving from the US, while I'm enjoying Paul Theroux' travel account … and just as we're about to read the first lines, what do we hear? Blaring from the main house!

# Patagonia: Country of the Winds

"Nowhere is a place."

*Paul Theroux, from: "The Old Patagonian Express"*

[km/miles 66,198/39,719 to 69,112/41,467| Chile Chico – Ushuaia]

*Great herds of guanacos move through Torres del Paine National Park in Chilean Patagonia.*

Soon after we cross the border to Argentina we reach the Ruta Nacional 40, an endless strip of dust running south at a safe distance from the Andes. We have long left Chile's lush, rampant green along the Carretera Austral behind us; here our world consists of thorny steppes, an infinite, windswept semi-desert under an equally infinite steel-blue sky filled with scudding scraps of ragged cloud. Lucy bounces easily over the rough washboard tracks, leaving a trail of dust visible for miles.

The region is devoid of people. The few settlements with gas stations are 200 kilometers (120 miles) and more apart, like islands in a sea of spiky grasses. While we were still on the Chilean side of the border in Chile-Chico we made sure to fill both diesel tanks to the brim, giving us enough gas to reach the next fuel stop at Tres Lagos where the RN 40 turns west to Lago Viedma. Or so we thought! Somewhere in the midst of this emptiness I switch over to Tank 2 and am stunned; the needle should show hard right on the display, but stops only one-quarter of the way over. What's wrong? Is the display faulty? Does the tank have a leak? Has a fuel hose split? Whatever; this scant drop of fuel won't take us to Tres Lagos. We drive off the road and examine the map. It shows a track running east 45 kilometers (27 miles) from here that ends up after a further 80 kilometers (48 miles) in Gobernador Gregores – where there is a gas station. We can make it that far. Gobernador Gregores has nothing of interest for passing visitors and is therefore ignored by the

guidebooks. Evening is falling by the time we arrive. We've had enough for the day, swallowed enough dust. We find a spot for the night on the premises of a *hosteria* on the edge of town, where we can shower in the communal bathroom. The night is astonishingly mild and windless. Somewhere nearby, music throbs into the early hours – no surprise in South America! The next morning we are at the gas station at nine. But only a few minutes before, the power in the whole village has been turned off for repairs to the power grid. We wait three hours for the power to come back on and the pumps to work. The tank barely takes thirty liters before it's full – so the problem was the faulty display after all, and we could have saved ourselves the detour to Gobernador Gregores.

Today we reach El Chalten, the northern gateway to Parque Nacional Los Glaciares. In this remote corner of South America the precise route of the border with Chile is still a matter for dispute; as a result, in the mid-1980s the Argentinians hastily threw together a new village on this spot before the Chileans had the same idea. El Chalten has all the provisional charm of a gold-rush town from the 19th century, and its inhabitants are probably driven by the same motives: grab what you can and high-tail it! Except their aim isn't to plunder gold mines, but to fleece tourists. Behind the village towers one of the most majestic mountains in all of South America, the Fitzroy Massif. Its vast granite pinnacles soar out of the plains like the turrets of a fairy-tale castle, attracting hordes of free

climbers and outdoor fans. But the rocky fortress is reluctant to show its face in the days we spend there. On the first evening it's revealed in the wan light of the setting sun, but during the night mighty banks of cloud pile up and spend themselves in a dramatic storm, impaling themselves on the sharp cusps of the massif. However, we're undeterred and hike along well-used trails to explore the mountain, traversing moss-grown woods and open savanna, past glacier-blue lakes and icy rushing streams. Again and again the

sun pokes its head out, but only for a few minutes at most. Once – at eleven at night – the clouds rip apart, parting like a curtain and revealing the stage of an unforgettable spectacle: we find ourselves gazing into a magnificent canopy of stars in the Patagonian night sky. The Milky Way curves in a vast arch from horizon to horizon. High in the sky rides the Southern Cross, a trusty guide. Then our gaze travels west and we can scarcely believe our eyes: an enormous comet lights up the night sky, gradually descending towards the massif and drawing a huge tail behind it. Transfixed by this spectacle of the heavens, we are overcome by an exhilarated reverie. It's as if everything we had experienced in the past months were compressed into a single moment, into a glowing dot of light in the firmament. Now we're utterly convinced that our journey is under a lucky star. To reach the southern end of the national park, we take

*A freehand self-portrait in Torres del Paine National Park*

*Trees in Tierra del Fuego are permanently crooked from the strong winds.*

*The sky over the Fitzroy Massif in Los Glaciares National Park presents a unique natural spectacle: that night, McNaught comet upstages the moon (right)*

a wide detour around Lago Viedma and Lago Argentino to Patagonia's tourist center, the town of El Calafate. It's strange that after spending hours wandering through the thorny, God-forsaken pampas, meeting barely a soul on our way, we end up that evening in a place where tourists from all over the world are strolling down tree-lined *avenidas* past coffee shops, fashion boutiques and souvenir stores. How the heck did all these crowds get here? Did someone finally invent beaming up while we weren't looking?

After spending a night at the town's campground, the next morning we head for the famous glacier of Perito Moreno, one of the few glaciers in the world which is still growing. Extending 30 kilometers (18 miles) into the Andean massif, the glacier's tongue forms a sheer seventy-meter (230 feet) cliff at the front, its craggy face glowing blue and pale green. Masses of pack ice press the tongue forward, creating enormous strain and making the glacier creak and groan like a giant's stomach. When it

calves, shedding blocks of ice the size of sky-scrapers to tumble into Lago Argentino, the noise can be heard for miles.

All afternoon we stand with countless other tourists on the viewing platform, unable to tear ourselves away from this breathtaking feast of sight and sound. We spend the night in the vis-itors' parking lot – it's actually prohibited, but the park-keepers don't seem to mind. Before go-ing to sleep we listen to Perito Moreno creaking and groaning; occasionally it roars thunderously, and occasionally we have the feeling that the earth is shaking.

Early in the morning before the sun has risen, I return to the wall of ice once again – but this time nobody else is there: it's just the glacier and me. It is bitterly cold. Gray clouds sail past, and the waters of Lago Argentino are gray too, but in the east the sky begins to turn pastel red. The sun slowly appears through the mountain slopes and ragged cloud, and as its hesitant fin-gers finally touch the mass of ice, they make Per-ito Moreno sparkle like a vast uncut diamond.

Hours later we're on the road again amid the de-serted, rolling arid steppes. Small herds of gua-nacos move through the vast expanse of land, with feral horses and ostrich-like rheas. We see a family of foxes frolicking at the edge of the track, and once we nearly run over an armadil-lo. Patagonia is still the country of adventure and adventurers. The story of the gunslinger duo Butch Cassidy and the Sundance Kid who once rode from Ohio to southern Patagonia to rob the bank in Río Gallegos fits the region as well as the story of Bodo, the friendly native of Ham-burg who has taken early retirement to cycle here alone. We meet him at a corrugated-iron rest stop in the empty pampas and chat a little. His greatest adversary, he tells us in carefully chosen words, is the endless, icy wind. There are days when he is forced to break off his ride be-cause he simply can't make headway against it; he has no choice but to pitch his tent at the side of the road and wait for calmer weather. Except, he adds with a grin, that pitching a tent in these winds is sometimes like trying to get water-lilies

Right: A solitary gaucho in the thorny plains of Patagonia. Bottom right: German heavies – travelers meet up at Fitzroy. Opposite page: Grumbling giant – Perito Moreno glacier.

A legend – Ruta 40

to flower in the desert. This said, he mounts his cycle and continues cheerfully on his way.

On the other side of the border between Chile and Argentina, the steppes abut onto a national park considered by connoisseurs to be among the most beautiful spots on the whole American continent: Parque Nacional Torres del Paine. Drought is not a problem here, as the puffy mounds of dark-gray Pacific clouds permanently obscuring the sky indicate. Half a dozen lakes crowd against a backdrop of craggy mountains with peaks that have iced over in the moist cold of this subpolar zone. "Pie-nee" – pale blue – was the Indians' name for the waters. And what an understatement! The only things that are pale about Lago Nordenskjöld are the whitecaps of its waves breaking on the shore. Further out, a magnificent landscape unfurls in rich oil-paint hues. From our campsite at Lago Pehoe we have a panoramic view of unearthly-seeming cliffs on the opposite bank. We clamber up narrow, steep trails to reach windswept heights and gaze down into a primeval natural world that is surely unique. Flamingos plow through the shallow water far below, faintly recognizable as thin pink brush marks in the leaden landscape. Above us in the dark-gray sky, condors circle majestically with never a wing beat. The granite pinnacles of Cerro Torre Grande, Paine Chico and Cuernos del Paine soar in the distance. The wind blows chill around our ears, and we have to fight to stand upright on the edge of the cliffs. This is untamed nature, experienced with all the senses: we are seeing, smelling, hearing and feeling its primordial might. Is this the crowning glory of creation? Its flawless, perfectly modeled masterpiece? "Nowhere is a place," wrote Paul Theroux about Patagonia. But he never came to Torres del Paine.

# Destination

In 1520, after weeks of searching for an east-west passage to the Pacific, the Portuguese explorer Fernando Magellan sailed through the straits that would later bear his name, steering his ship through icy waters under huddled banks of cloud past storm-lashed islets and dark cliffs; by night, he noticed a barren land to the south that was weirdly illuminated by flickering lights. What was it? Was it the fires of the Alakaluf, a tribe of nomadic seafarers? Or did Magellan see the nocturnal camps of the Sek'nam, a hunting people who primarily subsisted on guanacos? Or did the lights belong to the Haush people, who named themselves Manekenk? Magellan was destined never to find out; he never set foot on the soil of the mysterious island past which he sailed. But the name he gave it still conjures up dark fantasies today: Tierra del Fuego, the land of fire.

The ferry crossing from Punta Arenas across the Straits of Magellan to Porvenir takes two and a half hours. When we step onto the gray earth of Tierra del Fuego in the late afternoon, the weather is probably similar to that of 500 years ago – unpleasantly cold and rainy. A howling gale screams around Lucy and tears a hole in the covering of the scooter. We follow a rough track, hemmed in between the choppy ocean, sparse savanna and lowering sky, and head south. Our mood is as ambivalent as the Patagonian weather, swinging wildly between cheerful euphoria and glum melancholy. We're in Tierra del Fuego! We're practically straight on course for the final destination of our journey! Heck, we've made it! The thought makes us proud. And silent. We set up camp for the night in a broad bay with a stony shore, pull on our rain jackets and run a few hundred meters along the water to an abandoned fisherman's hut. Back in our heated cabin we heat up yesterday's leftover lentil stew and stare out into a world spreading before us like a black and white photograph in the endless twilight of these latitudes. Although dark and bleak, it is

We've done it: the unassuming end of the Panamericana

beautiful. That night temperatures fall to almost zero, and the restless winds claw at Lucy like snuffling monsters. "Lonely Planet" writes on Tierra del Fuego: "If you are wondering what it feels like to be at the end of the world, look no further …."

Tierra del Fuego was split up between Chile and Argentina by the simple expedient of a pencil line on a map. We cross the border the next day. In fact, we had intended to take more time over the last few hundred kilometers to Ushuaia, spending a few days at Lago Blanco and in the little town of Tollhuin on Lago Fagnano. But instead, we're impelled to move onward to the southern tip of the island, to the end of the road, to our goal. We first roar through scrubby grassland, half swept along and half impeded by the gale force winds, and then pass redbrown forests, reaching the most southerly town on earth around midday of the next day. We cross the town boundary of Ushuaia, steer Lucy – our faithful Lucy – through Calle Magellanes, turn left into Don Bosco and finally park in Calle San Martín in the heart of the city. We're here!

"Traveling is better than arriving" is a favorite motto of mine, but no arrival has ever been as sweet as today's. Around one and a half years ago, on August 15, 2005 to be precise, we were standing at Prudhoe Bay in Alaska near the polar sea, at the most northerly end of a rough trail. Then we glanced north one more time and climbed into Lucy, from then on heading south: onwards and onwards, through barren tundra, dark primeval forests, bone-dry savanna and hot deserts. Through glittering megacities, colonial towns, tranquil villages and wretched slums. We've crossed fifteen countries, 126 latitudes and four climate zones. We've plunged into valleys over one hundred meters (328 feet) below sea level and climbed mountain passes at altitudes of 5,000 meters (16,400 feet) above it. We've

*Solitary fisherman's hut at the Magellan Straits*

"cabaña" with a loft bed, kitchenette and open fireplace plus glorious views over the town and the Beagle Channel.

When Alejandro, our friendly landlord, hears our story, he makes us a gift of a bottle of wine for each night of our stay! And we stay ten nights altogether. Not because Ushuaia has so much to see (and no, not because of the free bottle of wine per day), but because at this point in the journey we have to draw a line, and because we want to take a break and stop for a while.

For the first time in months our table is stacked not with travel guides and maps, but with photos from Peru, flotsam from Mexico and souvenirs from Alaska. Our gaze is directed backwards, not forwards. We leaf through our diaries and spend hours reminiscing about almost-forgotten episodes ("hey, do you remember the stunned expression of that policeman in Guatemala when I told him to take his trousers off before he inspected Lucy ...").

There's still time for a little sightseeing. We visit the town's old jail, where the cells can still be seen. And the Museo del Fin del Mundo in one of Ushuaia's oldest houses, displaying stuffed animals, old photos, Indian cult objects and parts of wrecked ships from which fragments of the archipelago's natural and cultural history can be pieced together. The first white settlers did not arrive on the islands until 1860. Today it is estimated that at that time Tierra del Fuego had around 10,000 indigenous inhabitants. By 1910 this figure had dropped to only around 350. In only fifty years they had become practically ex-

driven on every possible type of road, from twelve-lane highways to narrow dirt tracks, fine sandy beaches and boggy swamps where we almost sank. Exactly 548 days and around 56,000 kilometers (33,600 miles) later, we've reached the southern end of the road. There's not much more beyond this point. A few more kilometers (miles) to the south-west, then a few little islands off Tierra del Fuego, and then nothing more than the icy ocean between us and Antarctica.

We get out and hold each other tightly for a long time. Then we look around. It would be a lie to describe Ushuaia's main street as an architectural treasure, but it has its own charm. And by luck or by fate, we promptly find ourselves standing in front of a pretty yellow-painted house which proves to be a fine restaurant. We go in, take a seat at a wooden table next to a cozy radiator and order a bottle of sparkling wine and "centolla", king prawns on salad, a regional specialty. I'm so bursting with the urge to share our story that soon the owner, the waitress and anyone who comes too close has heard all about it – and it's worth the telling! At the edge of Ushuaia we rent a tinct. A plaque in the small "Indigenas" section of the museum informs us that the Indians definitely did not die out from any violence meted out to them by the new settlers, but from the unfamiliar sicknesses introduced by the foreigners and from their own inability to adjust to the new culture. We read this and are struck dumb. Not a word that Indians were hunted down like animals, not a line about the times when bounty payments of one pound sterling were made for each dead Indian. The distortion of history in favor of Latin America's European immigrants sometimes takes on extremely tasteless forms.

Our regular haunt in Ushuaia is a little cafe in Calle Maipu which serves delicious sliced salmon on home-baked baguette, fine wines and wonderful "espresso corto". We spend hours in the inn, surrounded by the scent of warm bread, the black-haired waitress teaching us something of the fierce pride of Argentine women, and Astor Piazzolla's tango music resounding from the loudspeakers, as vibrant as the sea on the other side of the road – such a clichéd view of the region, but so absolutely real! These days do us so much good. We could carry on like this for weeks. I read an article which states, "As the 'island of the damned', Tierra del Fuego has long been considered the ultimate test of human endurance …." How could anyone in Ushuaia agree? Although it's true that while the town is certainly Argentine, it's not the true Tierra del Fuego.

To discover the real face of Tierra del Fuego, we have to leave the town behind us, driving south over bumpy dirt tracks to arrive at the oldest "estanzia", Haberton. In 1886 English settler Thomas Bridges established this sheep farm in solitary seclusion, and it is still run by his descendants today. We stroll through the old wooden buildings, visit the farm's own Museo Acatushun with an impressive collection of bones of Tierra del Fuego's marine mammals; we board a motor-boat which takes us to a tiny island with beaches populated by Magellan and Gentoo penguins. These delightful creatures show little fear; quite the contrary, in fact – when I lie in the sand to photograph them, some approach until they are only a few centimeters away, probably finding me as amusing as I do them. There I am lying flat on the ground with the penguins staring down at me, and I have the impression that this is re-adjusting the settings in the grand scheme of things. We continue west to Tierra del Fuego National Park, where the Panamericana finally peters out in the swampy ground. A sign at the end of the road puts the official seal on it: "Aqui finaliza la Ruta Nac No 3." We pose in front of it for the obligatory photo, and then wander along the silvery turquoise waters of Lago Roca to the Chilean border, which is unmarked by any boundary stone in this deserted wilderness. Dense mats of moss and muddy yellow swamps cover the terrain, next to the towering, knotty stacks of beaver colonies. Tierra del Fuego's brief summer is nearing its end. The sun still breaks through and floods the hillsides country with its dazzling, hard-edged light, but it no longer warms. The night we spend next to a glacial river is bitterly cold. It's time to leave Tierra del Fuego – this bleak patch of earth at the end of a magnificent continent. It's a long way home. We stand at the chilly waters of the Beagle Channel, glance briefly back to the south, climb into Lucy and head north …

*Who loves you, baby …?*

*Hacienda Haberton*

*Surprisingly high traffic on Tierra del Fuego's roads ...*

A masterpiece of creation: Torres del Paine National Park in Patagonia

# Argentina: Northward

"There is no end, everything is a constant new beginning."

Octavio Paz, Mexican author

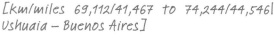

[km/miles 69,112/41,467 to 74,244/44,546|
Ushuaia – Buenos Aires]

If you want to get ahead, get a hat: encounter in El Bolsón, Argentine Lakes

Ruta 3 is the big sister of Ruta 40 along which we traveled to Tierra del Fuego, and runs north through eastern Patagonia close to the Atlantic shore. While also surrounded by arid steppes and thorny desolation like its dusty counterpart in the west, Ruta 3 is asphalted throughout. The road is almost deserted, except for our constant companion through the vast expanses of Patagonia – the strong south-westerly wind, which causes birds to fly backwards, the grassy steppes to ripple and crash like ocean waves, and Lucy to cruise along like a schooner in full sail. We are relaxed and serene as we rock along, no longer hurrying to reach a predefined destination, but now in the final throes of our journey. A dull, yet pleasantly languorous inner emptiness overtakes us, like the aftermath of a difficult examination after months of preparation or the completion of an important task after weeks of sleepless nights. Once the task is finished and the examination passed, one tends to fall into a kind of comatose vacancy – and that's precisely our state of mind as we make the smooth journey along Ruta 3.

Even the sun, such a rare visitor in recent weeks, shows its face again, surprising us around midday somewhere in the void between Puerto San Julián and its nearest neighbour of Caleta Olivia almost 400 kilometers (240 miles) further north. We stop at a parking bay, bring out our table and chairs and set them up in the midst of the pampas to enjoy a lavish meal of home-made marinated herb cheese, salami, olives from a jar, fresh baguette from the "panaderia" in

Puerto San Julián and a soupçon of Sauvignon Blanc. And then suddenly something happens out of the blue which was probably well overdue after a distance of over 67,000 kilometers (40,200 miles): Lucy won't start. The starter is ticking over and the batteries are OK, but the engine won't start. Is there a fuel blockage? An air blockage? All the lines are in order. I bypass one of our two diesel filters which had recently been causing some gasket problems, but to no avail. In any case all my fiddling around is only helpless activity for the sake of it, by someone who knows next to nothing about motor mechanics. Checking the repair manual under the heading "Troubleshooting," I'm confronted with rather bizarre sentences like "Use extractor tool T77F-4220-B1 to remove the thrust flange spacer (see Section 3.148). To do this, dismantle the drive pinion on the fuel pump shaft (using assembly tool T83-6316-B) and adjust steering to 1.5 ATDC for cetane number 47 or higher. In the event of difficulty – start walking, dumb ass."

Oh, Lucy, you might have picked a busier spot to break down. 50 kilometers (30 miles) to the next gas station and 150 (90 miles) to the nearest town worthy of the name. We lock up and take up a position at the edge of the road with the aim of hitch-hiking to the garage at Tres Cerros. Quite some time passes until a vehicle finally appears, a thirty-ton truck with an empty trailer. The truck comes to a standstill next to us and the cab door opens, disgorging Miguel. From Comodoro Rivadavia, 350 kilo-

meters (210 miles) away, he's overweight and mustached and, when he smiles, reveals a huge gap where other people have a front tooth – and he smiles a lot. He listens to our sorry tale, bends over Lucy's engine and performs a few mysterious actions – probably checking the hydromagnetic high-speed idling pump shaft flange, but I wouldn't swear to it.

After a while Miguel also gives up. We can't push-start Lucy because of her automatic transmission, so we agree that Miguel will tow us to Tres Cerros. Minutes later we're back on Ruta 3, this time as part of a king-size convoy: Miguel's 20 meter (66 feet) truck, our Lucy with her five and a half meters (18 feet), and 10 meters (33 feet) of towrope between us. A grand total of 35.5 meters (116 feet). Anyone planning to overtake us had better get up a good speed before attempting the maneuver.

*Above: Paul Theroux made it famous – the Old Patagonian Express .*
*Left: For Argentines, mate is far more than mere tea; for us, it's an acquired taste.*

*Orderly idyll:*
*Villa Angostura at*
*Lago Nahuel Huapi,*
*Argentine Lakes.*

Tres Cerros is a bare outpost of civilization, featuring a gas station, snack bar, a few dusty wooden stalls, seatless toilets – not a place you'd want to get stuck in. There is a mechanic, but it's Saturday and he won't be back till Monday. We're getting used to the idea of staying here over the weekend when Miguel shuffles up, bends over the engine again (with at least five Argentines following his every move: an open hood has the same attraction to an Argentine as an open beer hall to a Bavarian), tests a few lines once more, asks me occasionally to turn the ignition key … and lo and behold, Lucy's engine starts. What was wrong? I ask. No idea, he says and slurps his mate tea.

Lucy may have started, but the engine is stuttering and fitful. Miguel suggests we leave her running and follow him to Comodoro Rivadavia 300 kilometers (180 miles) away, where there is a garage specializing in Bosch diesel vehicles. We follow his advice, reaching the town

hours later after darkness and bidding our kindly Samaritan farewell in front of the garage. We try to press a hundred pesos on him, but he refuses, instead accepting a bottle of sparkling wine from our store of provisions and roaring off in his thirty-ton truck. A helping hand is never closer than in South America!

There's a campground only a few kilometers from the garage; we set up camp there in a sheltered spot and fall exhausted into our bunks after a scant meal. On Monday morning we bring Lucy (who starts with the utmost reluctance!) to the garage. By the afternoon she's purring like a pussycat. The problem actually was that the engine was getting insufficient air. What did I say! And if only I'd had assembly tool T83-6316-B, I could have done the whole thing myself … what the heck …!

We approach Buenos Aires in a wide arc, permitting ourselves a long detour to the west to visit Argentina's lakes – a return to the foot of

the Andes. When the mountains rise before us it's like a reunion with old friends. We stroll through sleepy, picturesque villages, fish in deserted crystalline lakes, stretch our hammock between ancient cypresses – rarely has our journey been so peaceful.

And then we embark on the last stage of our journey. Buenos Aires is said to be more European than any other city in South America. Well, let's see about that. The statistics tell a different story: 13 million inhabitants in Greater Buenos Aires, 18,000 buses (God help us!),

50,000 taxis, 190 theaters, 129 museums …. We toil along four to eight-lane arterial roads (it's not always easy to tell) through sleazy suburbs before we are finally ejected onto Avenida 9 de Julio, 125 meters (410 feet) wide and leading right into the heart of the city. In the center, only one street over from this impressive boulevard, we take a shabby room in a little hotel which we had already booked on the Internet in Ushuaia.

In ten days, "MS Grande Francia" sails from the harbor, and this Grimaldi Group freighter will convey us and Lucy back to Germany in an Atlantic crossing lasting over three weeks. We have ten days to complete the necessary formalities, and ten nights to explore Buenos Aires.

Amazingly, the first hurdle is passed after only half an hour's chat with friendly Inez at the shipping agency; since we are accompanying the "cargo," we don't need to visit the customs office or immigration before traveling; we don't need to fight our way through piles of incomprehensible, complicated red tape or bribe any officials. All we have to do is drive up to the ship

There's a knack to fishing …

Lago Nahuel Huapi near Bariloche

on the day of sailing – and that's it. How incredibly simple! But then we're no longer in Panama or Colombia!

And so we can devote ourselves all the more energetically to the second part of our plan. Le Corbusier described Buenos Aires as "a mistaken city, possessing neither a modern spirit nor a spirit of the past," because it strove to be European and therefore was never popular in America. We stroll down the Florida, the city's longest pedestrian zone and an avenue of consumerism that likens itself to Paris or London. Magnificent buildings from the early 20th century, gray with the fumes, soot and smoke of time, tell a story of a glorious past and its transitory nature. At Plaza de Mayo we step up to Argentina's political heart, the place where the independence from Spain was proclaimed, where Perón announced the decisions of his government, where the "porteños" – as the city's inhabitants call themselves – hailed the invasion of the Falkland Islands by their army in

1982 and the return of democracy in 1983. And every Thursday it is still the meeting-place of Argentina's highest-profile human rights group, the Mothers of Plaza de Mayo. Identifiable by the white headscarves they wear, they still demand explanations of the fate of their sons and husbands. During the military dictatorship between 1976 and 1983, 30,000 people "disappeared" in the regime's torture chambers.

At Plaza de la Republica we are impressed by the 67-meter (220 feet) obelisk, a plain stone column marking both the center of Buenos Aires and that of Argentina. A fenced-off construction site nearby blocks our entry to Teatro Colón, a majestic work of classical architecture with 3,000 seats and seven tiers.

Although we work our way through a packed program of Buenos Aires' obligatory tourist sights, the city fails to charm us. That happens elsewhere, more gradually, in quieter moments. Sipping an espresso in one of the countless corner cafés, for example, or browsing

in junkstores in the district of San Telmo, strolling through Palermo's tree-lined avenues and … yes, of course … evenings in shadowy tango bars blurred by red wine, where we sit at wobbly bistro tables before a splintery wooden stage on which elegantly clad actors bare nothing less than the sadness of their inner souls. What would Buenos Aires be without its tango? Once the music of the impoverished suburbs, the harbor taverns and bordellos in La Boca, soulful and very far from demure. The tango is "a melancholy thought which can be danced," said composer Enrique Santos Discepolo. While this aphorism is true, the comment attributed to George Bernhard Shaw is equally so: "Tango is the vertical expression of a horizontal desire."

On Sundays in broad daylight, the tango is danced in the cobbled streets of San Telmo – the men impeccably dressed in suits with oiled

Still in America …!

On the safe side …

hair, the women in high heels and occasionally well advanced in years. They glide with lascivious languor and tenderness and, despite the serious nature of the tango, with light steps. We lean against a house front and spend a long time watching the activity of the colorful crowds around us – dancers, singers, musicians, puppeteers, peddlers, natives sipping mate, tourists hoping for a bargain, police in bulletproof vests, pickpockets, beggars … A stage that is so different from the rest of Latin America – but so very un-European! While San Telmo lacks the grave resignation of the Andean uplands and the Caribbean abandon of Colombia, the indigenous spirituality of Guatemala and the puerile machismo of Mexico, it is nonetheless a natural element of the sensuous world reigning over this appealing, chaotic continent through which we have journeyed for almost eighteen months, and from which we will depart in a few days. On this Sunday afternoon, it seems, we fit the final piece into place in a puzzle which has occupied us since we crossed the border into Mexico in December

of the year before last. It is as if the continent is bidding us farewell in a buoyant, melancholy show, as if it were building us a bridge between America and Europe – a bridge of purest poetry.

So there we stand, marveling, smiling and soaking up the scene with all our senses. And we understand that every melody that is played, every song that is sung, every acrobatic trick performed and every dance completed is aimed at us alone and bears a single common title: "Nunca olviden!" – "Never forget!"

# Epilogue

Monday. This morning, on my way to the studio, I bought copies of my usual newspapers at the newspaper kiosk around the corner. "Monday special as usual, Mr Boyny?", commented the kiosk owner, wearing the greasy cap he has never been seen without since I started buying my newspapers from him – around a hundred years ago. He means well, no question of that, but I confess his "as usual" caught me off guard. We've only been back for a month, but already we seem to have slotted perfectly into a rhythm which has seamlessly persisted from the time before our great journey – according to some more people than my newspaper seller. I'm not sure how I should take it. Don't get me wrong. We didn't suffer any sense of frustration when we returned, turning Lucy into our street, parking outside the block, climbing to the fifth floor and opening our apartment door for the first time to be greeted by a room filled with coaxing afternoon sunshine, in which the plants were flourishing and even the windows

were sparkling clean. We didn't plunge into depression when we walked through our district for the first time and – how European – ordered our first Chianti at the Turkish restaurant under Gauloise umbrellas. We met easy-going, friendly people, accepted the city traffic as pleasantly harmonious and the affluence of our environment as an immense gift. It was good to be home! But gradually the questions began to form. What is left over after such a journey? How much of our flood of experiences and impressions can we retain and incorporate into our daily Munich routine? What's changed – and what hasn't? The place we returned to is still the same – and that's fine; our newspaper seller still wears the same old cap, the same charming cashier still works in the supermarket, and she still goes to the same unflattering hairdresser, Oscar Lafontaine is still working on his political comeback. And yet Germany has changed. "Rumpler," the restaurant on the corner, is no longer allowed to set up planters of flowers outside because a

Green city councilor – of all people – has a problem with them; our chancellor is now a woman and seems, at this point, to be making a pretty good fist of her job; a band composed of school kids called "Tokio Hotel" is causing acned teenage girls to collapse en masse; the newspapers carry articles about a tax surplus (!), and since the World Cup soccer championship, waving German flags is politically correct.

It's good to meet up with family, friends, neighbors and acquaintances. It does our hearts good to sit among people we know well, and – more important – who know us well. But when the casual question "How was it?" is asked, we find it hard to answer. It's not a question that can be answered in half a sentence, and anything longer is often too burdensome for our listeners. Travel stories are tiring – perhaps also frustrating – for those who stayed behind. And so we change the subject and chat about subjects closer to home like the latest health service reforms, the smelly compost bins in the yard and the national soccer league!

And yet our journey is present everywhere around us. More inwardly, it's true, but definitely a component of our daily lives. It has not retired to the background, but hovers in the room with us like a heavy scent – no… like a sweet fragrance that persists, refusing to be dispelled. We still see the pictures before us: the snowy peaks of the Andes in Bolivia, the ragged children in Nicaragua, our descent into the Grand Canyon, grizzlies in Alaska. These buried memories probably cast a different light on apparently normal circumstances at home, rearranging priorities of what is important and trivial and putting the cares of an affluent society into a different perspective.

I'm fully aware that these are not new ideas. As the saying goes, if an ass goes traveling he will not come home a horse. How true that is! We came back from our journey no smarter than

we were when we left. In our two years of travel between Alaska and Tierra del Fuego, we came no nearer to answering life's big questions. But perhaps we're now better at asking some of the right questions.

At any rate, "as usual" definitely has no place here! And what a shame it would be, indeed. Unpacking the boxes we had stored in Lucy and which are now stacked in our hall, I came across a crumpled scrap of paper bearing a comforting sentence which I scrawled down from a glass case in the Visitor Center of Denali National Park in Alaska at the start of our journey. It ran:

"A mind that is stretched by a new experience can never go back to its old dimension." Could someone please translate that for my newspaper seller?

Free to new experiences …

Bedding down for the night off the highway near Hanksville, Utah

# Further Titles of Interest

**China**
200 pages, 320 illustrations,
ISBN 978-3-7658-1672-7
ordering code 81672

**Colors of the Tropics**
176 pages, 250 illustrations,
ISBN 978-3-7658-1691-8
ordering code 81691

**Kalahari – Wild Africa**
200 pages, 300 illustrations,
ISBN 978-3-7658-1593-5
ordering code 81593

**The Earth as Art**
300 pages, 380 illustrations,
ISBN 978-3-7658-1628-4
ordering code 81628

**Forest Planet**
208 pages, 230 illustrations,
ISBN 978-3-7658-1689-5
ordering code 81689

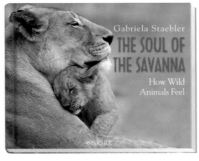

**The Soul of the Savanna**
176 pages, 200 illustrations,
ISBN 978-3-7658-1673-4
ordering code 81673

www.bucher-publishing.com

**ᐅB BUCHER**

# Impressum

**Michael Boyny**, born 1963, is a freelance photographer whose main professional focus has been on travel and food. His work has taken him to every continent, and his award-winning reports have appeared in books and magazines around the world. He lives in Munich, but stays on the road: for him, travel is an addiction. More information is available at www.boyny.de

This work has been carefully researched by the author and kept up to date as well as checked by the publisher for coherence. However, the publishing house can assume no liability for the accuracy of the data contained herein.

We are always grateful for suggestions and advice.
Please send your comments to:
Bucher Publishing
Product Management
Infanteriestr. 11a
80797 Munich, Germany
e-mail: editorial@bucher-publishing.com

Translation: Alison Moffat-McLynn, Munich, Germany
Proofreading: Elizabeth Harcourt, Picton, Canada
Design: Frank Duffek, Munich, Germany
Cartography: Astrid Fischer-Leitl, Munich, Germany

Product management for the English edition:
Dr. Birgit Kneip
Product management for the German edition:
Joachim Hellmuth
Production: Bettina Schippel
Technical Reproduction: Repro Ludwig, Zell am See, Austria
Printed and bound in Italy by Printer Trento

**See our full listing of books at**
**www.bucher-publishing.com**

ISBN 978-3-7658-1657-4